Cheat Sheet #1: How to Make the Most of This Book

osCommerce is a free, publicly-licensed Amazon-style online ecommerce store program. Store owners or website developers who want to quickly have an inexpensive, easy-to-use, powerful online store that they can administer themselves through a control panel in their browser should:

1. Plan to start your first OSCommerce store with as close to the standard, or "default" configuration as possible.
2. Get yourself a technical guru who will install your store for free if you host with them - see the Appendix for a list of installers, consultants and hosts.
2. Fill out the **Pre-Setup Checklist,** Chapter 1.
3. Then run through the **Quick Start Guide**, Chapter 2.
4. Use the rest of this manual only as you need it.

This book is intended to be a handy reference for osCommerce so you can figure out what you can comfortably tackle by yourself, and what you should leave to a technical pro. See **Appendix A** for a list of installers, consultants and web hosts who are ready to help you.

LIST OF FREE CHEATSHEETS INCLUDED:
Cheat Sheet #1: <u>**How to Make the Most of This Book**</u>
Cheat Sheet #2: <u>**PRE-SETUP Checklist for Your Store**</u>
Cheat Sheet #3: <u>**InfoBox Checklist**</u>
Cheat Sheet #4: <u>**Greetings and Menu Bars Checklist**</u>
Cheat Sheet #5: <u>**Advanced Users' Stylesheet Cheatsheet**</u>
Cheat Sheet #6: <u>**Advanced Users' Cheat Sheet**</u>

All Cheatsheets can be found on the web as easy forms that you can save or receive by email and forward to your installer or technical pro. See Appendix B for the web address of all Cheatsheets.

Icons used in this book:

 TIP: This is something important that will make your project go much easier.

 **CAUTION: Follow directions exactly, this is easy to mess up!**

TECHNICAL STUFF: Unless you love the technical stuff, this is something that a programmer or other technical person should do.

DANGER, WILL ROBINSON! Don't do this unless you really, really know what you are doing!

OSCOMMERCE USERS MANUAL:A GUIDE FOR STORE
OWNERS AND WEBSITE DEVELOPERS

OsCommerce Users Manual:

A guide for store owners & website developers

oscommerce users manual:
*a guide for store owners and
website developers Version 2.0*

©2004 Kerry Watson
Pithy Productions, Inc.

Printed in Canada

Second Printing: August, 2004

TRADEMARKS

All terms mentioned in this book that are known to be trademarks or service marks have been appropriately denoted. Pithy Productions cannot attest to the accuracy of the information. Use of a term in this book should not be regarded as affecting the validity of any trademark or service mark. osCommerce is released under the GNU Public License. Pithy Productions is a trademark of Pithy Productions, Inc.

WARNING AND DISCLAIMER

About the Author

Kerry Watson joined the Open Source movement in 1996 as a consultant for Netscape working as the Producer for the Netscape Navigator website. Her mission was to make Netscape accessible to everyday users, not just technical users, and she wrote plain-language tutorials such as Netscape Navigator for Internet Explorer Users and Netscape Tips & Tricks. Before that she was a vice president of NetAdvantage, an e-commerce turnkey outsourcing company like PayPal. She holds an MBA and a Bachelor's of Liberal Studies with a concentration in Sociology and Communication. Today she heads Pithy Productions, Inc., a web project management company that specializes in custom OsCommerce websites.

Acknowledgements

I couldn't have written this book without the generous help and support of my wonderful family, Patrick and Jessica. I am grateful for your love.

Dedication

This guide is dedicated to you, the long-overlooked user--the store owner or web developer. Because programmers may build the world, but users *inhabit it*.

Your Feedback is Appreciated

I welcome your comments! Please feel free to email me to let me know what helped and what didn't, or what you'd like to see covered in future editions.

Please note that I cannot help you with technical problems related to the topic of this book. Due to the volume of mail I receive, I might not be able to reply personally to every message.

Sincerely,

KERRY WATSON
osc@pithyproductions.com

Contents

Part II: Store Maintenance

OsCommerce Users Guide
Introduction

If you've just had your osCommerce store installed and want to open quickly for business, your grand opening is just a few clicks away.

Who this book is for:

If you are a store owner or website developer who wants a powerful, Amazon-style online store installed so you can easily administer it yourself using the administrative module in your browser, this book is for you.

This guide is designed for people with little or no technical experience, but who have a technical support person to call on for help, such as their installer. Advanced users may occasionally have to insert one carefully-explained line of code into a file. See the back of this book for installers who can help you.

This book is intended to be a handy reference so you can figure out what you can comfortably tackle yourself, and what to leave to a technical pro.

What is osCommerce?

osCommerce is a free, powerful, Open Source*, "Amazon.com"-like e-commerce program. It can be used almost immediately out of the box within 30 minutes of installation, by a store owner or web developer with no PHP programming experience using only your web browser and this book. It can be modified, customized, and have bells and whistles (called "contributions" because they are contributed for free) added by programmers.

osCommerce's Out-of-the-Box Features include:

For Customers:
Set up customer accounts
Customer address books (other shipping destinations)
Order history
Shopping carts—both Temporary (not logged on) and permanent (logged on)
Search the catalog for products or manufacturers
Product reviews written by customers
E-mail notification of new products
Number of products in each category listed
Bestseller lists
Display customers who bought this also bought...

For Shop Owners:
User-friendly administration using your web browser
Add/Edit/Remove categories, products, manufacturers, customers, and reviews
Statistics for products and customers
Tax zones, classes, and rates
Payment and shipping modules link to popular payment processors and shippers
Multi-Currency and Multi-Languages
Backup tool
Many add-on options available

Tips for using this book

1. If possible, plan to start your first OsCommerce store with as close to the standard, or "default" configuration as possible. Once it is up and running to suit your needs, you can add a bell here or a whistle there, one at a time. Start small and grow big.

2. Whether you are a store owner new to the Internet, or a programmer with many years of experience, **fill out the Pre-Setup Checklist** completely before you start any osCommerce website. This will allow you to have all the information about the website in one place. This will save

---

* "Open Source" software is software whose code is available for users to look at and modify freely. Many popular Internet programs are open source, including Linux, PHP, MySQL and Apache servers.

you many, many hours of back-and-forth figuring out little, "just-one-more" things that were staring you in the face all along.

3. Then **run through the Quick Start Guide.** This will get you set up and operating in as little as 30 minutes.

4. Finally, go through the rest of this manual as you need it, or refer to it at your leisure. There is no reason to read every section. Wait until you have a specific need—like "hey, this field is too small; how do I make it bigger?"—then satisfy that need.

What about installation?

This guide specifically does *not* include a section on installation of your osCommerce website. There are many web hosts that will install your default osCommerce website for free if you host with them. Why struggle when you can get it installed for free?

The main reason that installation and setup of a PHP website with a MySQL database are not included in this book because it is an *advanced topic* in programming. There is a separate database to install, permissions to set, and many parts that can go wrong. There is no reason for most store owners or web developers to muck into such a technical job. If you absolutely must tinker with everything yourself, get my companion book, the **osCommerce Technical Manual** at www.oscommercemanuals.com.

Icons used in this book:

I have used a number of special icons to make using this book easier. They are as follows:

 TIP: This is something important that will make your project much easier.

 CAUTION: Follow directions exactly, this is easy to mess up!

 TECHNICAL STUFF: Unless you love the technical stuff, this is something that a programmer or technical person should do for you.

DANGER, WILL ROBINSON! Don't do this unless you really, really, really know what you are doing!

TIP: At the end of their lives, nobody ever wished they had spent more time at work.

Pre-Setup Checklist

These questions must be answered to set up your store correctly the first time. It will save you lots of time later if you take the time now to answer every one. Advanced web developers or installers can use the answers to quickly zip through the installation.

NOTE: This can also be found on the web in an easy-to-use form that you can email to yourself or your installer. See the Appendix for the web address.

Each Item number below corresponds to the number on the next page, the "default" osCommerce setup:

GENERAL

	Your Answer:	Cheat Sheet *for developers/installers:*
1. What do you want to be the Page Title that shows in your top browser bar?		index.php
2. What domain name do you want for this store?		For correct server setup.
3. What do you want to name your company logo that will be placed in the top left corner in place of the OSCommerce logo?		images/oscommerce.gif about Line 19 in includes/header.php Also change the alt text of the image from "OSCommerce" to the new logo name.
4. In addition to the top gray navigation bar, do you want an additional navigation bar above the top gray navigation bar? If so, list the link names.		create html table file such as "catalogheader.htm" and upload it to **includes** directory. NO head, body or other tags. Add this to approx. line 55 of includes/header.php: <? Include "catalogheader.htm");?>
5. OSCommerce includes navigation pictures for My Account, Cart Contents, and Checkout. Do you wish to use these?		See detail pages.

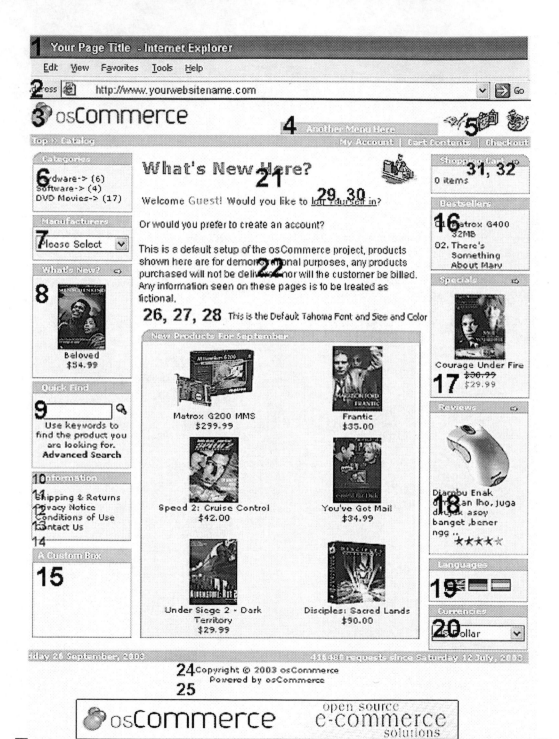

1 Your Page Title - Internet Explorer

Edit   View   Favorites   Tools   Help

2 ress   http://www.yourwebsitename.com   Go

3 osCommerce

4 Another Menu Here   **5**

Top >> Catalog   My Account | Cart Contents | Checkout

Categories

6 rdware-> (6)
Software-> (4)
DVD Movies-> (17)

Manufacturers

7 Please Select

What's New?

8

Beloved
$54.99

Quick Find

9

Use keywords to
find the product you
are looking for.
Advanced Search

10 Information

11 Shipping & Returns
12 Privacy Notice
Conditions of Use
13 Contact Us
14

A Custom Box

15

21 What's New Here?

29, 30 Welcome Guest! Would you like to log yourself in?

Or would you prefer to create an account?

22 This is a default setup of the osCommerce project, products
shown here are for demonstrational purposes, any products
purchased will not be delivered nor will the customer be billed.
Any information seen on these pages is to be treated as
fictional.

26, 27, 28 This is the Default Tahoma Font and Size and Color

New Products For September

Matrox G200 MMS
$299.99

Frantic
$35.00

Speed 2: Cruise Control
$42.00

You've Got Mail
$34.99

Under Siege 2 - Dark
Territory
$29.99

Disciples: Sacred Lands
$90.00

Shopping Cart   **31, 32**
0 items

Bestsellers

16 01. Matrox G400
32MB
02. There's
Something
About Mary

Specials

17 Courage Under Fire
$38.99 $29.99

Reviews

18 Djambu Enak
dan lho, juga
druk asoy
banget ,bener
ngg ..
★★★★☆

Languages

19

Currencies

20 Dollar

riday 28 September, 2003   416480 requests since Saturday 12 July, 2003

24 Copyright © 2003 osCommerce
Powered by osCommerce

25

osCommerce   open source
e-commerce
solutions

LEFT-COLUMN: Do you want to include the following boxes or pages?		To remove:
6. Categories		Put // in front of file name in file includes/column_left.php
7. Manufacturers		Put // in front of file name in file includes/column_left.php
8. What's New		Put // in front of file name in file includes/column_left.php
9. Quick Find		Put // in front of file name in file includes/column_left.php
10. Information:		Put // in front of file name in file includes/column_left.php
11. Shipping & Returns		Put // in front of file name in file includes/column_left.php
12. Privacy Notice		Put // in front of file name in file includes/column_left.php
13. Conditions of Use		Put // in front of file name in file includes/column_left.php
14. Contact Us		Put // in front of file name in file includes/column_left.php
15. Custom:		create a table in an html file such as "newbox.htm" and upload it to **includes** directory. NO head, body or other tags. Add in the appropriate position in includes/column_left.php: <? Include ("newbox.htm");?>
RIGHT-COLUMN: Do you want to include the following boxes or pages?		To remove:
16. Bestsellers		Put // in front of file name in file includes/column_left.php
17. Specials		Put // in front of file name in file includes/column_left.php
18. Reviews		Put // in front of file name in file includes/column_left.php
19. Languages		Put // in front of file name in file includes/column_left.php
20. Currencies		Put // in front of file name in file includes/column_left.php
MIDDLE COLUMN: 21. Do you want to change the heading		includes/languages/english/index.php, be sure to put a forward slash before

that reads, "What's New Here?"

any apostrophe like this "What\'s" or your page will break

22. What text do you want to be placed below "What's New Here? (approx. 250 words or less)

includes/languages/english/index.php search for define('TEXT_MAIN', ' ' and insert text between the two ' '

23. Do you want to include the following box: New Products for (Month)

Put // in front of file name approx. line 316 in file index.php

PAGE FOOTER:

24. Do you want a copyright statement for your own company?

add table html to includes/footer.php

25. Do you want to run affiliate banners in your footer?

add table html to includes/footer.php

SECTION 2. COLORS & STYLES
FONTS:

26. The default font STYLE is Tahoma font. Do you want to change this font style?

stylesheet.css

Do a global replace for "font-family: Tahoma,"

27. The default font SIZE is 12 pixels. Do you want to change this font size? (note: substantially changing the size may change all column widths and layouts of your pages)

stylesheet.css

Do a global replace for "font-size: 12px;"

28. The default font COLOR for plain text is black. Do you want to change this font color?

stylesheet.css

Do a global replace for "font-size: 12px;"

29. The default LINK COLOR is black that changes to gray when you put the mouse over it. Do you want to change these link colors?

stylesheet.css

Search on the color number you want to replace

30. The default LINK STYLE is underlined. Do you want to remove the link underlines?

stylesheet.css

Replace text-decoration for A and A:hover

LOOK AND FEEL:

31. The default menu bar color is gray. Do you want to change this menu bar color?

change color of TD.headerNavigation, TD.footer, TD.InfoBoxHeading, .productListing-heading. TIP: search for the color number instead.

32. The default shape of menu bars is rounded corners. Do you want rounded corners or square?

Copy images/infobox/corner_left.gif, corner_right.gif, and corner_right_left.gif. Create anti-aliased images in the same color as the menu bar color. TIP: upload a clear gif with the same file name.

OPTIONAL: MY STORE TEXT

My Store is store settings that will be displayed on different pages throughout the website. You may also do it yourself using the Administrative Module in the Administration-My Store section. If you include it here for your installer, he or she may insert it for you.

NOTE: The following items are NOT shown on the attached picture.

From main Administration Module, select Configuration, My Store, and enter it in the appropriate line.

33. What is your store name?

Enter it in the appropriate line.

34. Who is the store owner?

Enter it in the appropriate line.

35. What email address do you want customers to email to?

Enter it in the appropriate line.

36. What email address do you want to be displayed as the FROM: address when you send emails to customers?

Enter it in the appropriate line.

37. What country is your

Enter it in the appropriate line.

store in?

38. What state is your store in?

Enter it in the appropriate line.

39. Do you want an email notification to be sent to you each time you receive an order?

Enter it in the appropriate line.

40. What is your store's address and phone number?

41. How many decimal places do you wish to show when calculating tax?

Enter it in the appropriate line.

OPTIONAL: PAGE TEXT

There are 4 default pages in the Information Box in the LEFT-COLUMN that need your customized text filled in. If you include it here for your installer, he or she can insert it for you.
NOTE: These are NOT shown on the attached picture..

From the main Administrative Module, select Tools-Languages-Define Languages section.

42. What do you want to say on the Shipping & Returns page?

In Administration-Tools-Define Languages, open shipping.php and copy the text to the appropriate place.

43. What do you want to say on the Conditions of Use page?

In Administration-Tools-Define Languages, open conditions.php and copy the text to the appropriate place.

44. What do you want to say on the Contact Us page?

In Administration-Tools-Define Languages, open contact_us.php and copy the text to the appropriate place.

45. What do you want to say on the Privacy Notice Page?

In Administration-Tools-Define Languages, open privacy.php and copy the text to the appropriate place.

SECTION 3.
CUSTOMIZATION AND IDENTIFICATION
NOTE: These are NOT shown on the attached picture.

46. Do you have a large number of products that need to be entered?

EZPopulate or other add-on contribution can be used to batch upload files. Ask your installer for details.

47. What username and password do you want

Install .htaccess or a login contribution.

to use for the Administration screen?		
48. What is your name?		For contact purposes.
49. What is your email address?		For contact purposes.
50. Do you already own this domain or do you need your installer to get it for you?		For setup.
51. Do you want custom matching buttons to match your website's look and feel?		For setup.
52. Is there anything else you need to tell your installer about your website?		For setup.

osCommerce Quick Start

What's in this chapter?

After you have filled out your Pre-Setup Checklist and had your store installed, you are ready to do a Quick Start. This chapter shows the store owner or website developer how to:

1. Log on
2. Use the main administration menu
3. Set the settings that will be used throughout the store
4. Enter your product categories, then product information
5. Set up credit card and shipping
6. Set up your location and tax information, and
7. Set informational messages (privacy, contact, shipping & returns).

Level of difficulty: easy.

If you have any difficulty, turn to the detailed chapters of this book, or contact your installer.

1. Log on for the first time

1. Open your browser (usually Internet Explorer) and type the web administration address that your installer gave you. It will probably look like this:

> `http://www.yourstorename.com/catalog/admin/`
> or `http://www.yourstorename.com/admin/`

NOTE: This is usually abbreviated as "**/catalog/admin/**" in the rest of this book.

2. If you received a username and password, enter them and press **Enter**.

TIP: If your store administration does NOT require a username and password, that is like leaving your stockroom door open to customers.
DANGER: If there is no password required, your installer MUST install password access for you. Contact the installer of your store and ask them to install either "htaccess" or an "osCommerce contribution" (add-on) to limit administrative access to you and those you choose.
IMPORTANT: The first first time you log onto your store, you should change your password. KEEP YOUR PASSWORD IN A SAFE PLACE. Your installer can easily assign you a new password if he or she uses .htaccess, but it is *impossible* if they use the current version of "Admin Access Levels" add-on contribution.

2. Use the Main Administration Menu

After you enter your password, you will come to the "**Main Administration menu**" where we will work through the following **five areas** during your Quick Start. You will return to this **main Administration Menu** each time you finish a section.

1. My Store: Set up Global Store Settings

2. Catalog: Enter Product Info

3. Modules: Link to Credit Card, Shipping

4. Locations/ Taxes: Set Location & Taxes

5.Tools: Set Messages on Main Page, Privacy, Contact, Shipping & Returns

Figure 1
"Main Administration Menu"
Each section in the Quick Start Guide begins and ends here

3. Set the "My Store" Settings

"**My Store**" in the **Configuration menu** is where you tell your store its new name, your name, email address, and other details that will be displayed throughout many areas throughout the program.

To get to the My Store Menu:

To get to the My Store Menu from the **Main Administration Menu**, click **My Store**.

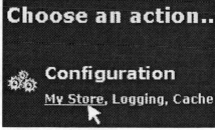

Figure 2
Main Administration Menu

My Store

Title	Value	Action	Store Name
Store Name	osCommerce	▶	edit
Store Owner	Harald Ponce de Leon	ⓘ	
E-Mail Address	root@localhost	ⓘ	The name of my store
E-Mail From	osCommerce <root@localhost>	ⓘ	Date Added: 02/12/2004
Country	United States	ⓘ	
Zone	Florida	ⓘ	
Expected Sort Order	desc	ⓘ	
Expected Sort Field	date_expected	ⓘ	
Switch To Default Language Currency	false	ⓘ	
Send Extra Order Emails To		ⓘ	
Use Search-Engine Safe URLs (still in development)	false	ⓘ	
Display Cart After Adding Product	true	ⓘ	
Allow Guest To Tell A Friend	false	ⓘ	
Default Search Operator	and	ⓘ	
Store Address and Phone	Store Name Address Country Phone	ⓘ	
Show Category Counts	true	ⓘ	
Tax Decimal Places	0	ⓘ	
Display Prices with Tax	false	ⓘ	

Figure 3
The Configuration Menu's "My Store" Section

For detailed information about each item on the screen, find the **Action** column and click the **"i"**, then click the **EDIT button** in the right column to see the detailed explanation and make changes.

TIP: If you are still not sure about an item after reading about it in this Quick Start section, turn to the detailed section of this manual or ask your installer for help.

At a minimum, be sure to review and set the following My Store items:

My Store

Title	
Store Name	Your Store's Name.
Store Owner	Your Name.
E-Mail Address	Your Email address.
	When you send emails, the "From" address,
E-Mail From	usually yours.
	Your Country, for shipping/tax purposes.
Country	For shipping/tax purposes.
Zone	
Expected Sort Order	
Expected Sort Field	
Switch To Default Language Curre	
Send Extra Order Emails To	If you want to receive an email each time an
Use Search-Engine Safe URLs (st development)	order is placed.
Display Cart After Adding Product	
Allow Guest To Tell A Friend	
Default Search Operator	
Store Address and Phone	Your Store's Address and Phone.
Show Category Counts	
Tax Decimal Places	How many decimal places you want, usually
Display Prices with Tax	two, otherwise it will display 4 or more.

Figure 4
The Configuration Menu's "My Store" Detail—
Items to Edit during Quick Setup

After you finish editing your **My Store items,** return to the Main Administration Menu by clicking **"Administration"** in the **top gray navigation bar:**

Figure 5
Clicking the word "Administration" in this TOP NAVIGATION BAR returns you to the Main Administration Menu.

4. Enter your product and category information

In this section you will enter your all product information into the Catalog. First you set up your product categories, then you can enter the product information.

 TIP: Do you have dozens or hundreds of products and images to enter? If so, there are add-in products, called "contributions" that can add your products and images in one batch. Ask your installer to set it up for you.

To enter product and category information, from the **main Administration menu,** click **Catalog.**

Figure 6
Main Administration Menu

This brings you to Catalog Categories/Products. There are 3 sample test categories already in there to get you started:

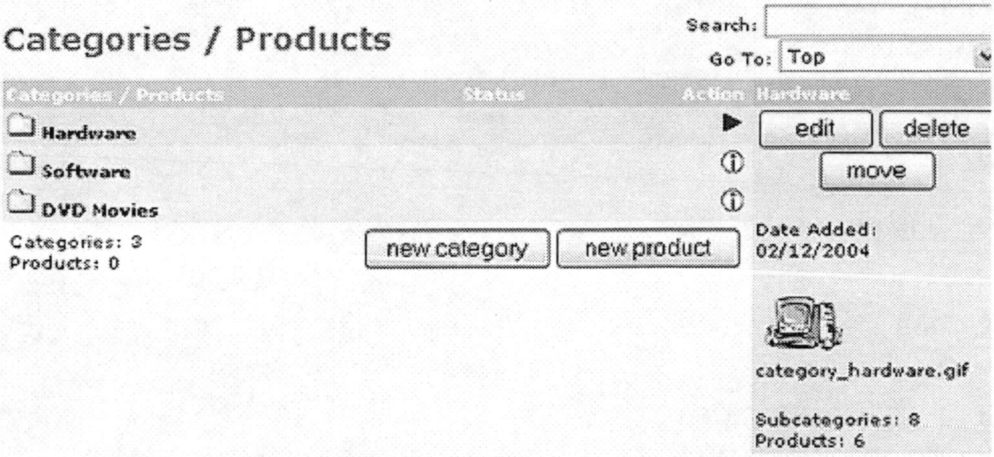

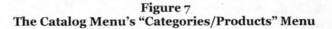

Figure 7
The Catalog Menu's "Categories/Products" Menu

TIP: Click the sample test categories and select the "EDIT" button to see how they are set up, but be sure to DELETE the sample categories before your store goes live.

TIP: Enter ONE category and ONE product to test your site, THEN enter the remaining products when you know you have done it properly.

Adding your first Category:

Before you can add your own products, you must first **create a Category** for it:

Click the **"NEW CATEGORY" button** and fill in the appropriate information.

If you want this category to be listed FIRST in your category listing, enter the number "1" in the Sort Order box:

Figure 8
The Catalog Section's
"New Category" Menu

Adding your first new product:

After you have finished adding your first product category, **SELECT it by clicking the new category FOLDER.** Then you can add your first new product to your new category.

IN THE APPROPRIATE CATEGORY, Click "NEW PRODUCT".

CAUTION: **If you forget to click Category first, your products will not show up in the Category listing of your website! You will have to re-enter or move them into the correct category.**

If you need to set product sizes, colors, or other attributes, turn to the PRODUCT MANAGEMENT chapter or contact your installer for help.

5. Link to Credit Cards and Set Shipping

For your customers to pay online, you need to link to a third-party online credit card processor. If you already have a credit card processing account, osCommerce can automatically link to many credit card processors, including the popular and easy PayPal.

From the **main Administration menu,** click **Modules.**

Modules
Payment, Shipping

Figure 9
Main Administration Menu
Modules Section

This brings you to Payment Modules. This is a list of **third-party credit card processors** that can be automatically installed. Click the "**i**" symbol and then the **Install** button to install.

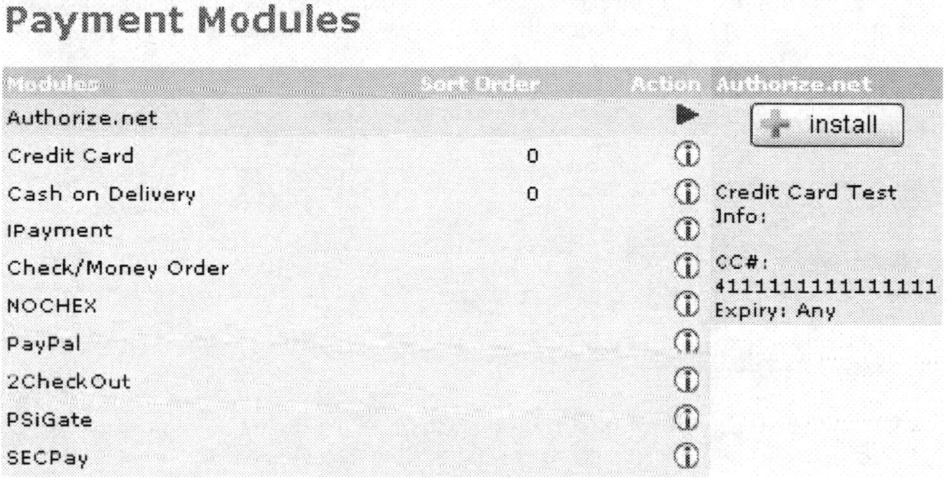

Payment Modules

Modules	Sort Order	Action	Authorize.net
Authorize.net		►	install
Credit Card	0	ⓘ	
Cash on Delivery	0	ⓘ	Credit Card Test
IPayment		ⓘ	Info:
Check/Money Order		ⓘ	CC#:
NOCHEX		ⓘ	4111111111111111
PayPal		ⓘ	Expiry: Any
2CheckOut		ⓘ	
PSiGate		ⓘ	
SECPay		ⓘ	

Figure 10
The Module Menu's "Payment Modules" Menu

TIP: You must *first* **open an account with one of the companies listed in order to process your payments through them.**

To install a payment module, simply click the **Install** button and enter the account information from your credit card processor. If you need detailed assistance turn to the Payments Chapter.

The "Credit Card" module allows you to process credit cards manually, but it MUST BE INSTALLED ON A SECURE SERVER so credit card numbers get encrypted. Get your installer to do this.

TIP: The third-party credit-card processors use secure servers, so you may not have to. Check with your processor to be certain.

TIP: If you do not see your credit card processor listed, your installer can probably install an add-on module called a "contribution." Contact him or her for details.

Next Set Up Shipping

osCommerce can calculate your shipping costs for you. For shipping to be automatically calculated, you need an account with a shipping company. osCommerce automatically links to many shippers, including Fedex, USPS, and UPS.

To set up shipping, from the main Administration menu, click **Modules**, then **Shipping. OR** just select **Shipping.**

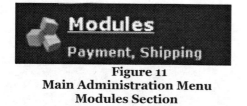

Figure 11
Main Administration Menu
Modules Section

This brings you to Shipping Modules. Here you will find a list of shipping companies that can be automatically installed, and an explanation of what is needed to complete the process:

Shipping Modules

Modules	Sort Order	Action	United States Postal Service
Flat Rate	0	ⓘ	install
Per Item		ⓘ	
Table Rate		ⓘ	United States Postal Service
United Parcel Service		ⓘ	You will need to have registered an account
United States Postal Service		▶	with USPS at http://www.uspsprioritymail.com/et_regcert.
Zone Rates		ⓘ	to use this module

Figure 12
The Module Menu's "Shipping Modules" Menu
With US Postal Service Selected in the "Action" Column

TIP: Click each of the modules and select EDIT to see how they are set up. Select the shipper and shipping modules that best fit your needs.

If you need additional assistance in setting up your shipping, turn to the Shipping Chapter of this book or contact your installer for help.

6. Locations and Taxes

You must specify a location for your store so osCommerce can calculate the correct tax when someone orders from an area in which you are required to collect taxes.

In order to charge the correct tax for your location, you must set your correct tax information in three steps:

1. Tax Zone (*where*)
2. Tax Class (*what*), and
3. Tax Rate (*how much*).

It's not difficult if you do it in this order.

Check with your accountant or lawyer so you know exactly what taxes to charge.

Set Location

From the main Administration menu, click **Tax Zones**

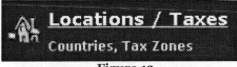

Figure 13
Main Administration Menu
Locations/Taxes Section

This brings you to the Tax Zones section. This is Step 1, the *"where"* you will charge tax.

Tax Zones

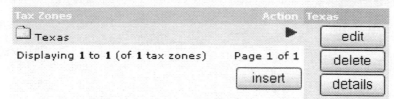

Figure 14
The Locations/Taxes Menu
Step 1 of 3 Tax Zones Menu

 TIP: Notice the left-hand menu... there are Zones, and then there are Tax Zones. Do not confuse the two! You want TAX ZONES.

A sample state is entered in the normal installation as a sample tax zone for you. You MUST delete this or all Floridians you ship to will be charged tax on your products!

Add your new Tax Zone:

Click **INSERT**, then enter a name and description of your new Tax Zone:

Figure 15
Locations/Taxes
Tax Zones Menu

Click **Insert** again to save. If you must collect taxes for local, city or elsewhere, repeat for each tax zone.

Add a new Tax Class:

This is Step 2 of taxes, the *"what"* you will charge tax on. Click **New Tax Class**. Enter the Name and Description of what you need to tax.

Taxable Goods

| edit | delete |

Date Added:
02/12/2004
Last Modified:
02/12/2004

Description:
The following types of
products are included
non-food, services, etc

Figure 16
Locations/Taxes
Step 2 of 3 Tax Class Menu

Add a new Tax Rate:

This is Step 3 of taxes, the *"how much"* you will charge for each tax. Click **New Tax Rate** to add a new rate:

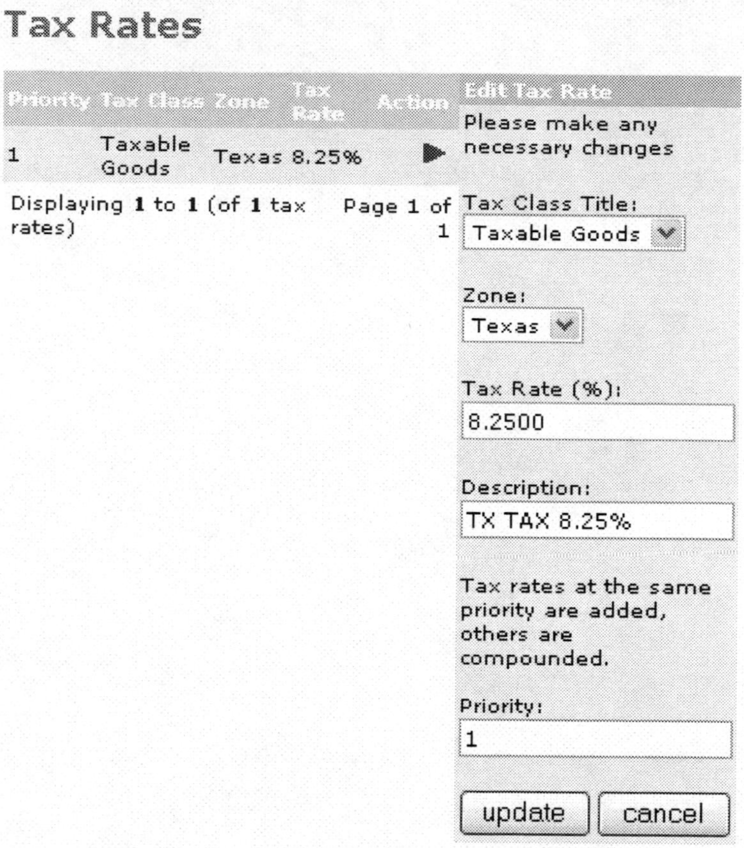

Tax Rates

Priority	Tax Class	Zone	Tax Rate	Action
1	Taxable Goods	Texas	8.25%	▶

Displaying **1** to **1** (of **1** tax rates)   Page 1 of 1

Edit Tax Rate

Please make any necessary changes

Tax Class Title:
Taxable Goods ▾

Zone:
Texas ▾

Tax Rate (%):
8.2500

Description:
TX TAX 8.25%

Tax rates at the same priority are added, others are compounded.

Priority:
1

update   cancel

Figure 17
The Locations/Taxes Menu's
"Tax Rates" Menu

5. Set Informational Messages

The **Tools section** of the **Main Administrative Menu** is where you enter the informational text that goes on your home page Welcome paragraph, the Shipping and Returns page, Conditions of Use, Privacy Policy, and Contact Us. In the Tools section we will go to the **File Manager** to manage these files.

 CAUTION: Follow directions exactly, this is easy to mess up!
ALWAYS MAKE A BACKUP FIRST!!!

TIP: To make drafting your messages easy, first write them in a Word Processor such as Word or WordPerfect. When they are perfect, follow these directions carefully to paste them into the appropriate document.

Inserting the text in the right place is the trickiest part of a standard installation, so if you have any difficulty, contact your installer for help.

TIP: There are Add-On text editors that your installer can install for you so you do not have to see ANY computer code while you are editing. Ask your installer to install an "HTML Area" contributions, or refer to the appendix.

If you are using a different version such as osCommerceMAX, CRE Loaded 6.0, or any version other than osCommerce MS2.2, you MUST CONTACT YOUR INSTALLER. FOLLOW THEIR INSTRUCTIONS ON EDITING TEXT EXACTLY. THESE INSTRUCTIONS APPLY ONLY TO STANDARD OSCOMMERCE, NOT TO ANY OTHER VERSION.

Take a look at each of these webpages on your newly installed website to see where the text you are writing will go, usually an address like this or consult your installer:

`http://www.yourwebsitename.com/catalog/index.php`

1. The Home Page "welcome" paragraph
2. The Shipping & Returns information in the "Information" InfoBox
3. The Conditions of Use information in the "Information" InfoBox
4. The Privacy Policy information in the "Information" InfoBox
5. The Contact Us page in the "Information" InfoBox.

To insert your informational text that goes on your home page welcome, the Shipping and Returns page, Conditions of Use, Privacy Policy and Contact Us, from the **main Administration Menu,** click **Tools.**

Figure 18
Main Administration Menu
Tools Section

This takes you to the **Tools Sub-Menu,** which you will see listed in the **Left-Hand column.** Look for the **FILE MANAGER** in the left-hand column and click the words **FILE MANAGER** . This brings you to the **File Manager section**.

Select the pages to edit

The files you need to edit are all in the folder **catalog/includes/languages/english.** Click the **YELLOW FILE FOLDER** named **includes,** then click the **YELLOW FILE FOLDER** named **languages**, then click the **YELLOW FILE FOLDER** named **english.**

From here you may insert your text of any of the following documents listed by clicking the **document name** and clicking the **EDIT** button.

NOTE: There are more files in this folder, however, for illustration purposes only the five files you need to edit are shown here:

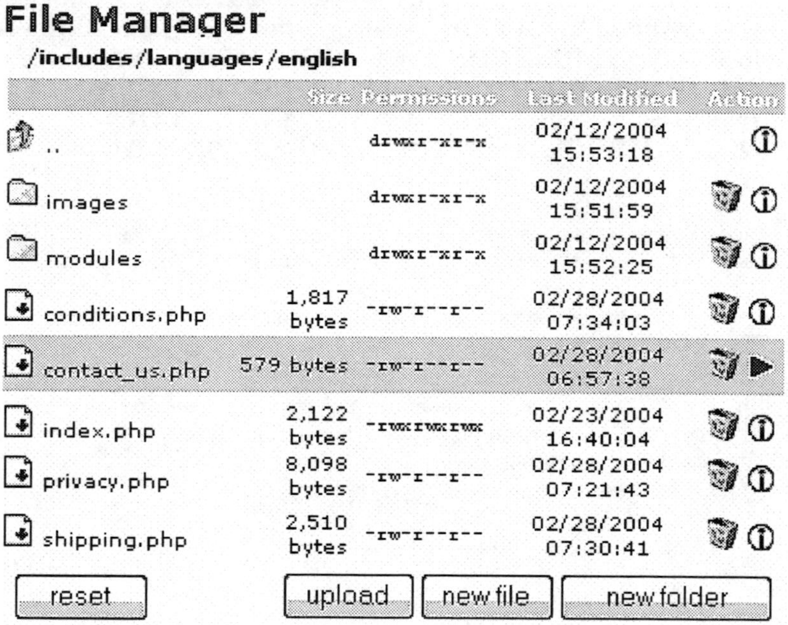

File Manager

/includes /languages /english

	Size	Permissions	Last Modified	Action
..		drwxr-xr-x	02/12/2004 15:53:18	①
images		drwxr-xr-x	02/12/2004 15:51:59	🗑 ①
modules		drwxr-xr-x	02/12/2004 15:52:25	🗑 ①
conditions.php	1,817 bytes	-rw-r--r--	02/28/2004 07:34:03	🗑 ①
contact_us.php	579 bytes	-rw-r--r--	02/28/2004 06:57:38	🗑 ▶
index.php	2,122 bytes	-rwxrwxrwx	02/23/2004 16:40:04	🗑 ①
privacy.php	8,098 bytes	-rw-r--r--	02/28/2004 07:21:43	🗑 ①
shipping.php	2,510 bytes	-rw-r--r--	02/28/2004 07:30:41	🗑 ①

[reset]   [upload] [new file] [new folder]

Figure 19
The TOOLS menu File Manager page, where you insert your text into the five documents listed

FILENAME	PAGE NAME
conditions.php	The Conditions of Use page.
contact_us.php	Contact Us page.
index.php	Your Home Page "Welcome" paragraph.
privacy.php	Privacy Policy.
shipping.php	Shipping & Returns information.

 STOP: MAKE A COPY OF YOUR FILE USING NOTEPAD BEFORE YOU START TO EDIT. If you accidentally move or remove any of the code, contact your installer. He or she can install a fresh copy of the page. DO NOT ATTEMPT TO FIX THE PHP CODE YOURSELF!

CAUTION: **You must paste your information EXACTLY over the highlighted area on the text below. You cannot move or remove anything, including the ' '); that surround your text, or the page will not work. THIS IS THE MOST COMMON MISTAKE PEOPLE MAKE, overtyping the ' '); that surround your text.**

After you click the document filename, you will see a document like the following sample below. **DELETE ONLY the highlighted text** and **PASTE** your information in its place:

conditions.php

```php
<?php
/*
 $Id: conditions.php,v 1.4 2002/11/19 01:48:08 dgw_ Exp $

 osCommerce, Open Source E-Commerce Solutions
 http://www.oscommerce.com

 Copyright (c) 2002 osCommerce

 Released under the GNU General Public License
*/

define('NAVBAR_TITLE', 'Conditions of Use');
define('HEADING_TITLE', 'Conditions of Use');

define('TEXT_INFORMATION', 'Put here your Conditions of Use information.');
?>
```

Figure 20
The conditions of use document: cut ONLY the
highlighted text and paste your text in its place

> **TIPS for PHP Editing: If you want a break between lines of your text, add one break symbol, like this:
**
> **If you want two breaks between lines, add two break symbols, like this:

**
> **To use an apostrophe (like what's)in your text, you must insert a forward slash \ before it so the program does not think it is a command. Example: what\'s**

Continue drafting your five pages in your word processor, save each as text, then Cut and Paste them into the appropriate documents.

What we covered in this chapter:

This chapter tells the store owner or website developer how to use the administration module to quickly set up their store, including settings that are used throughout the store, product information, credit cards and shipping, taxes and informational messages.

Your store should be ready for its grand opening! If not, refer to the detailed chapters or consult your installer for help.

Chapter

3

osCommerce Look and Feel

Now that your store is up, a few custom tweaks of the look and feel will make it uniquely yours.

In this chapter:

In this chapter we play with the things that make the store look and feel different. We start with the stylesheet – a page that sets the look and style of the website, we show you how to change your page background color and buttons, and modify the rounded corners of the top right and left infoboxes.

Fill out the **Look and Feel Checklist** and give it to your installer, or use it to make your own stylesheet editing a breeze.

Level of difficulty: medium

TIP: Stylesheets separate the "words" from the color and style. You edit the color and style of the words in this section, and the actual words in another section.

What is a Cascading Stylesheet?

The look and feel of the entire website is set by one page that specifies how each item is to be displayed—colors, sizes, styles, and backgrounds. This is called a cascading style sheet, or just style sheet.

Cascading Style Sheets are a godsend to every overworked, underpaid web developer. Write down the styles you want once, and those colors and styles "cascade" throughout your entire website for you. You can change the look of the whole website with one keystroke. No need to go back to every single page if you decide to change the look of the website!

The osCommerce stylesheets defines approximately 52 different styles, from important to minutia. If you want to change any color or style of font, heading, background, or link, this is where you or your installer does it.

To Edit Your Stylesheet

Your website's stylesheet is located in the top folder of your store's website as **stylesheet.css.** This is usually found at:

    http://www.yourstorename.com/catalog/stylesheet.css

You can edit **stylesheet.css** in Notepad, Wordpad, Microsoft Front Page, Dreamweaver, or any HTML editor software program that you feel comfortable using. You can also edit it manually using the File Manager in the TOOLS section of the Main Administrative Module. Consult the Tools Chapter for detailed instructions.

TIP: TO MAKE CHANGING YOUR STYLES EASY, simply answer the Styles Checklist in this book, then give your answers to your installer. You can also find this Styles Checklist online at www.oscommercemanuals.com/cheatsheets/

TIP: How do you know the numbers of the colors you like? Simply go to this page and play with the magic color selector:
`www.oscommercemanuals.com/cheatsheets/colorselector.html`

TECH-TYPES may download a "fully commented" copy of my stylesheet to make editing easier. This means that each style listed has a comment that describes what it does. Get it at www.oscommercemanuals.com/cheatsheets/OSCstylesheet22ms2-commented.css

Changing Page Background Colors

In a nutshell, osCommerce uses white page **backgrounds** because they are the easiest color to manage. Changing **page background colors** is one of those things that may seem simple, but can become incredibly expensive and complex. This is because images like buttons and product photos generally look best displayed on a clean white background. Many images have jagged edges (called "aliasing") that show up on other colors, but are not visible on white.

If you think you want to change the background color of the whole website, first have a quick test page done to see how it looks. It doesn't have to be pretty; simply the color of background you are considering with a few of your product photos and some buttons and graphics dropped onto it.

You can use the test page to estimate the cost of changing the rest of the site. You will probably need product photos and graphics specially made for that color background. Your graphic artist will probably need to re-create each image on an image background that matches your page background.

Unless you have oodles of money and time and patience, or lots of programming experience, you should stick with white page colors, at least for managing your first osCommerce website.

Changing Website Icons or Images

You may or may not like those extra icons or images for My Account, Cart Contents, Checkout, etc., that come pre-loaded in osCommerce. Changing them is so easy! Open your website in your browser, right-click on the image, and select Properties. The Properties panel tells you exactly where the image is located. To change or remove the image, simply upload a new image or a clear 1x1 pixel image in that exact location, giving it the same name as the image you want to overwrite.

Changing Buttons

osCommerce comes pre-loaded with standard buttons like the following:

Figure 21
Standard button style

The buttons are pretty, but the style is showy and colors work best if you have a dusty blue website.

The default buttons can all be replaced with buttons of your own choosing. If you are handy with graphics you can make them yourself, otherwise consult your installer for help finding a graphics artist to do it for you.

All button images are located in the following directory:

`catalog/includes/languages/english/images/buttons/`

Next Page: Figure 22
Buttons included in Default Installation

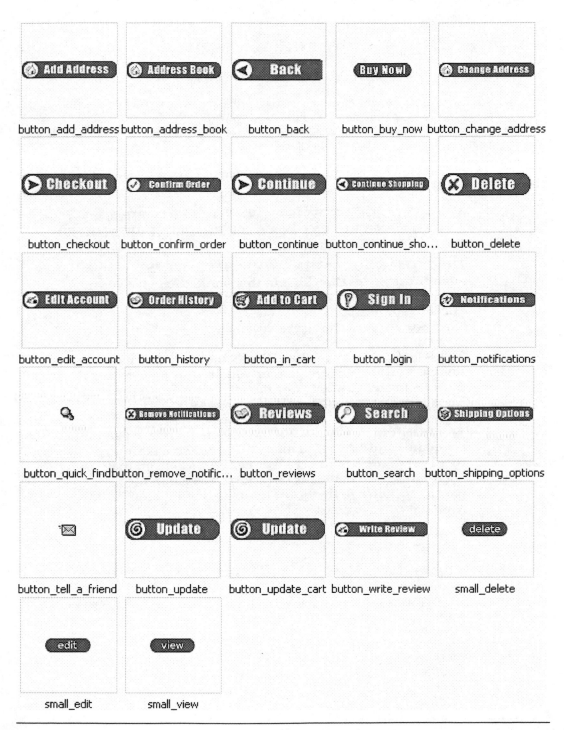

| button_add_address | button_address_book | button_back | button_buy_now | button_change_address |

| button_checkout | button_confirm_order | button_continue | button_continue_sho... | button_delete |

| button_edit_account | button_history | button_in_cart | button_login | button_notifications |

| button_quick_find | button_remove_notific... | button_reviews | button_search | button_shipping_options |

| button_tell_a_friend | button_update | button_update_cart | button_write_review | small_delete |

| small_edit | small_view |

Customizing the Default Buttons

If you have some graphics skills, the easiest way to change the color of your default buttons is:

1. Save each button with the dusty blue as the transparent color. Be sure to keep the exact filename, pixel size and extension (.gif).
2. Now you can just change the background layer color to the desired color and save them all again.

Of course you can always create your own unique custom buttons. Again, be sure to keep the exact filename, pixel size, and extension (.gif).

ALWAYS MAKE A COPY BEFORE YOU BEGIN EDITING ANY FILE AND KEEP IT IN A SAFE PLACE! NEVER, NEVER WORK ON THE ORIGINAL!

TIP: TO MAKE CHANGING YOUR STYLES EASY, simply answer the Styles Checklist in this book, then give your answers to your installer. You can also find this Styles Checklist online at
http://www.oscommercemanuals.com/cheatsheets

TIP: Those who are not artistically inclined may have their default buttons customized for you or your own custom buttons made. Contact your installer or refer to the list of installers and consultants in the Appendix.

You DON'T have to reinvent the wheel--there are pre-made templates and "skins" in many different styles, some of them very fancy. Some are free contributions on the osCommerce website, others are sold as complete packages. Refer to the list of template companies in the Appendix.

Customizing the Rounded Infobox Corners

If you change the colors of the page menus, you will find that the images of the top right and left rounded corners remain gray. You will need some minor graphics skills and a program like PhotoShop to change the color of these boxes, otherwise get an artsy friend to do it for you.

The rounded corner image files are located in the catalog/images/infobox/ directory, and the 3 file names are corner_left.gif, corner_right.gif, and corner_right_left.gif.

To change the rounded infobox corners,

1. Save each corner with the gray as the transparent color. Be sure to keep the exact filename, pixel size and extension (.gif).
2. Now you can just change the background layer color to the new menu bar color and save them again.

Look and Feel Summary

osCommerce's look and feel comes from the style sheet and the buttons.

Whether you customize it yourself, have someone else do it, or use pre-made templates or skins, be sure to fill out the Styles Checklist at

        http://www.oscommercemanuals.com/cheatsheets/look_and_feel

You can customize your own buttons, or you can get button add-ons or "contributions" from the osCommerce website.

Chapter

4

Customizing Your Header

Headers can range from your company logo, to elaborate schemes with complex navigation.

In this chapter:

The default installation of osCommerce includes a logo image in the header which most folks can easily replace with their own company logo. This is recommended for most new users.

The section in this chapter on adding a custom header is mostly for web developers. If you have any difficulty, contact your installer.

Level of difficulty: changing your logo is fairly easy; creating a custom header with navigation is difficult.

Using Your Company Logo as a Header

To replace the osCommerce logo with your own company logo, simply get a copy of your company logo in "gif" format, name the copy "oscommerce.gif", and copy it to the images directory as "catalog/images/oscommerce.gif".

 TIP: The size of the original osCommerce image is 204 by 50 pixels, but it seems to accept almost any size logo.

Making a Custom Header with or without a Navigation Bar

Custom headers are moderately easy for someone with some html experience. If you have made a navigation bar before in html, you will do fine here. If not, contact your installer.

CHANGING YOUR HEADER IN FIVE EASY STEPS

1. Create a separate html file for your header and menu system, using tables for placement.

2. Copy the "**body code**" only to the header file—no HTML, HEAD, TITLE, or BODY tags. This is because osCommerce will have already loaded those codes for you in PHP.

3. Name your file something easy to remember like "**catalogheader.html**" and put it in your main catalog directory.

4. Use an "images" directory while creating your file, then upload those images to the "images" directory of your osCommerce catalog.

5. Now add one line of PHP code to approximately line 55 of the file catalog/includes/header.php as follows (be sure to copy this exactly):

```
<? Include ("catalogheader.html"); ?>
```

Figure 23
Inserting the custom header into file
catalog/includes/header.php

TIP: If you use an HTML editor like DreamWeaver or Front Page, first get your header working perfectly in the editor, then manually remove it from between the body tags <body> </body> in Step 2.

Chapter
5

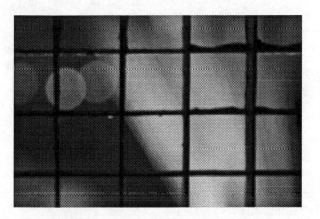

Customizing Your Left Column

Where we learn about InfoBoxes.

In this chapter:

You don't have to do anything with this chapter if you don't want. However, if you simply must remove one or more of the boxes in the left column, fondly known as "Infoboxes," to be happy, this chapter tells you how. You can also remove files from the "Information" Infobox such as the Conditions of Use page, or move Infoboxes from this column to the right column and vice versa.

Level of difficulty: This section is for web developers who are comfortable replacing one line of existing code using exact instructions.

osCommerce comes with a standard list of boxes in the left column, called InfoBoxes. It includes:

INFOBOX NAME	DESCRIPTION
Categories	The product category listing and quantity of items in each category. If you only sell one category of items, you won't need this box.
Manufacturers	Listing of manufacturers you have listed in the Administrative Module's Catalog section. If you are the manufacturer, of course you don't need this box.
What's New?	This is automatically updated by osCommerce with the most recent items you added in the Administrative Module's Catalog section. It is a matter of personal choice to keep it or not.
Quick Find	This is a search engine that searches only your website. Because it can find items that folks can't navigate directly to, I don't recommend removing it.
Information	This is standard information that every customer needs. Some is even required; for example, the privacy notice must state how you are going to use your client's private information and whether you will disclose or sell it to other parties.

Removing an Infobox

 **Only change one infobox at a time, then test your website to make sure your edit had the intended effect. BE SURE TO MAKE A BACKUP COPY BEFORE EDITING ANY FILE.**

To remove an Infobox you will simply "comment out" the unwanted box by inserting a php "comment" command. This way, if you wish to return the infobox at a later date, or if you made a mistake, you only need to remove the "comment."

TIP: Use "Find" or "Search" to jump to the exact phrase you want to edit.

To remove the Categories Infobox:

Open file **http://www.yourstorename.com/catalog/includes/column_left.php** and

Change this line	`include(DIR_WS_BOXES . 'categories.php');`
To	`// include(DIR_WS_BOXES . 'categories.php');`

To remove the Manufacturers Infobox:

Open file includes/column_left.php and

Change this line	`include(DIR_WS_BOXES . 'manufacturers.php');`
To	`// include(DIR_WS_BOXES . 'manufacturers.php');`

To remove the What's New? Infobox:

Open file includes/column_left.php and

Change this line	`require(DIR_WS_BOXES . 'whats_new.php');`
To	`// require(DIR_WS_BOXES . 'whats_new.php');`

To remove the Quick Search Infobox:

Open file includes/column_left.php and

Change this line	`require(DIR_WS_BOXES . 'search.php');`
To	`// require(DIR_WS_BOXES . 'search.php');`

To remove the Information Infobox:

Open file includes/column_left.php and

Change this line	`require(DIR_WS_BOXES . 'information.php');`
To	`// require(DIR_WS_BOXES . 'information.php');`

Adding or Removing Pages within the Information Infobox:

Information

Shipping & Returns
Privacy Notice
Conditions of Use
Contact Us

Figure 24
Information Infobox files

If you want to remove any of the pages within the Information Infobox, you will comment out the file name in the file **includes/boxes/information.php**

TIP: Use "Find" or "Search" to jump to the exact phrase you want to edit.

TIP: You can use this same technique to *add* files to the Information InfoBox.

To remove the Shipping & Returns page from the Information Infobox:

Open file includes/boxes/information.php and

Change this line	`'<a href="' . tep_href_link(FILENAME_SHIPPING)`
To	`//   '<a href="' . tep_href_link(FILENAME_SHIPPING)`

To remove the Privacy Notice page from the Information Infobox:

Open file includes/boxes/information.php and

Change this line	`'<a href="' . tep_href_link(FILENAME_PRIVACY)`
To	`// '<a href="' . tep_href_link(FILENAME_PRIVACY)`

To remove the Conditions of Use page from the Information Infobox:

Open file includes/boxes/information.php and

Change this line	`'<a href="' . tep_href_link(FILENAME_CONDITIONS)`
To	`// '<a href="' . tep_href_link(FILENAME_PRIVACY)`

To remove the Contact Us page from the Information Infobox:

Open file includes/boxes/information.php and

Change this	`'<a href="' . tep_href_link(FILENAME_CONTACT_US)`

line	
To	`// '<a href="' . tep_href_link(FILENAME_CONTACT_US)`

To move infoboxes into the left column from the right column:

Open file includes/column_left.php and in the place you want the moved box to show,

To move Languages, add this line:	`include(DIR_WS_BOXES . 'languages.php');`
To move the Currencies infobox, add this line:	`include(DIR_WS_BOXES . 'currencies.php');`

Then turn to the next chapter on Changing the Right Column and follow the instructions on removing the appropriate Infobox from that column, or both will appear.

Chapter

6

Customizing Your
Right Column

In this chapter:

Like the previous chapter, you don't have to do anything with this chapter if you don't want.
However, if you simply must remove or move one or more of the boxes in the right column, fondly
known as "Info boxes", this chapter is for you.

Level of difficulty: This section is for web developers. If you have any difficulty, contact your
installer.

osCommerce comes with a standard list of information boxes in the right column. Unlike the left column, some of these boxes display on the home page, others display on your products pages.

The standard Infoboxes in the right column includes:

INFOBOX NAME	DESCRIPTION
Shopping Cart	This is required for you to be able to sell anything; it has become standard for the cart to be in the top left. It is not recommended that you move it.
Bestsellers	This is automatically updated by osCommerce with the most frequently purchased items. It helps customers to know what's hot. It is a matter of personal choice to keep it or not.
Specials	Specials that you have designated in the Administrative Module's Catalog section. It is a matter of personal choice to use this section or not, but if you do, you must maintain it or your store will look out of date.
Reviews	Your clients can write reviews of your products and recommend them to others. This can be very powerful, however, you must maintain it regularly. It is a matter of personal choice.
Languages	If you have designated alternate languages on your website, this allows your website to be displayed in the alternate languages. If you only use one language, you should remove it.
Currencies	If you accept other currencies, this allows your prices to be displayed in other currencies. If you only accept one currency, you should remove it.
Tell a Friend	This is displayed on products pages, allowing a visitor to send an email to a friend recommending your product.
Product Notifications	Displayed on products pages, this allows customers to be added to a mailing list so you can notify them whenever you update a product.
Manufacturer Info	Displayed on products pages, if you have designated manufacturer info, you can include links to the manufacturer website.

Removing an Infobox

 **Only change one infobox at a time, then test your website to make sure your edit had the intended effect.**

To remove an Infobox you will simply hide the unwanted box by using a php "**comment**" command. This way, if you wish to return the infobox at a later date, or if you made a mistake, you only need to remove the "comment."

 TIP: Use "Find" or "Search" to jump to the exact phrase you want to edit.

To Remove the Bestsellers Infobox:

Open file includes/column_right.php and

Change this line	include(DIR_WS_BOXES . 'best_sellers.php');
To	// include(DIR_WS_BOXES . 'best_sellers.php');

To Remove the Specials Infobox:

Open file includes/column_right.php and

Change this line	include(DIR_WS_BOXES . 'specials.php');
To	// include(DIR_WS_BOXES . 'specials.php');

To Remove the Reviews Infobox†:

Open file includes/column_right.php and

Change this line	require(DIR_WS_BOXES . 'reviews.php');
To	// require(DIR_WS_BOXES . 'reviews.php');

To Remove the Languages Infobox:

† Not recommended.

Open file includes/column_right.php and

Change this line	`include(DIR_WS_BOXES . 'languages.php');`
To	`//    include(DIR_WS_BOXES . 'languages.php');`

To Remove the Currencies Infobox:

Open file includes/column_right.php and

Change this line	`include(DIR_WS_BOXES . 'currencies.php');`
To	`//    include(DIR_WS_BOXES . 'currencies.php');`

To Remove the Tell a Friend Infobox:

Open file includes/column_right.php and

Change this line	`include(DIR_WS_BOXES .` `'tell_a_friend.php');`
To	`//    include(DIR_WS_BOXES .` `'tell_a_friend.php');`

To Remove the Product Notifications Infobox:

Open file includes/column_right.php and

Change this line	`include(DIR_WS_BOXES .` `'product_notifications.php');`
To	`// include(DIR_WS_BOXES .` `'product_notifications.php');`

To Remove the Manufacturer Info Infobox:

Open file includes/column_right.php and

Change this line	```include(DIR_WS_BOXES . 'manufacturer_info.php');```
To	```// include(DIR_WS_BOXES . 'manufacturer_info.php');```

To Move Infoboxes into this Column:

Open file includes/column_right.php and in the place you want the moved box to show,

To move What's New, add this line:	```require(DIR_WS_BOXES . 'whats_new.php');```
To move the Quick Search infobox, add this line:	```require(DIR_WS_BOXES . 'search.php');```
To move the Information infobox, add this line:	```require(DIR_WS_BOXES . 'information.php');```

Then don't forget to turn to the previous chapter on Changing the Left Column and follow the instructions on Removing the appropriate Infobox, or both will appear.

Chapter

7

Customizing Your Middle Column

In this chapter:

The middle column contains several key items, including the main page welcome paragraph, main page text, and a listing of the most recent products you added to the products database.

Level of difficulty: This section is for advanced web developers. If you have any difficulty, contact your installer.

Only change one infobox at a time, then test your website to make sure your edit had the intended effect.

TIP: Use "Find" or "Search" to jump to the exact phrase you want to edit.

Changing the Greeting Text, "What's New Here?"

To change the wording of this greeting, follow the directions below. NOTICE the forward slash used before any apostrophe: not adding a forward slash is the most common cause of php errors.

Open the file catalog/ includes/languages/english/index.php and

Search for this line	define('HEADING_TITLE', 'What\'s New Here?');
and change it to	define('HEADING_TITLE', 'Whatever You Want to Say Here');

Changing the Greeting Text "Welcome, Guest! Would you like to log yourself in?

To change the wording of this greeting, follow the directions below. Be very careful not to touch the PHP codes.

Open file includes/languages/english/index.php

Search for this line	'TEXT_GREETING_GUEST'
and change only the text shown in bold red:	define('TEXT_GREETING_GUEST', 'Welcome <span class="greetUser">Guest!</span> Would you like to <a href="%s"><u>log yourself in</u></a>? Or would you prefer to <a href="%s"><u>create an account</u></a>?');

Changing the Main Page Welcome Paragraph

TIP: this text may be edited 3 different ways:
1. (Easiest) Using a WYSIWIG (what-you-see-is-what-you-get) add-in or "contribution" called TEXTAREA, which your installer will need to install for you;
2. (Medium) Using an editor like Dreamweaver or Front Page, then copying and pasting the text into the File Manager; or
3. (Advanced) Directly editing it with the Administrative Module's Tools-File Manager as shown below.

TIP: If you draft your main text in an html editor such as DreamWeaver or Front Page, copy and paste only the code as shown below. Do not copy the codes for HTML, HEAD, TITLE, or BODY.

To change the wording of the main page welcome text, follow the directions below. Be very careful not to touch the PHP code.

Open file includes/languages/english/index.php and

Search for this line	define('TEXT_MAIN','
and change only the text shown in **bold:**	define('TEXT_MAIN', '**This is a default setup of the osCommerce project, products shown are for demonstrational purposes, \any products purchased will not be delivered nor will the customer be billed**... \ **If you wish to download the solution powering this shop, or if you wish to contribute to the osCommerce project, please visit the \<a href="http://www.oscommerce.com" target="_blank">\<u>support site of osCommerce\</u>\</a>. This shop is running on osCommerce version \<font color="#f0000">**' . PROJECT_VERSION . '**\\</font>**.');

Removing the New Products for (month) Infobox

To remove this Infobox you will simply "comment out" the unwanted box. In the case of this particular Infobox, it will be a familiar HTML command, rather than PHP. This way, if you wish to return the infobox at a later date, or if you made a mistake, you only need to remove the "comment marks."

To remove the new Products Infobox:

Open file includes/column_left.php and

Change this line	`<tr><td><?php include(DIR_WS_MODULES . FILENAME_NEW_PRODUCTS); ?></td></tr>`
To	**`<!-- <tr><td><?php include(DIR_WS_MODULES . FILENAME_NEW_PRODUCTS); ?></td></tr> -->`**

Chapter

8

Customizing Your Footer

Good news, you have a lot of flexibility with the footer, and it is easy to edit.

In this chapter:

The footer can be edited by web developers or store owners who can use an HTML editor such as DreamWeaver or Front Page. If you have any difficulty, contact your installer.

Level of difficulty: easy.

TIP: Remember, your osCommerce public license requires that you leave the osCommerce copyright statement intact.

Figure 25
The osCommerce Footer

Adding a Company Copyright, navigational links, or other edits to the footer

To add a copyright, navigational links, or make other edits to the footer, simply do the following:

1. Start your html editor (DreamWeaver, Front Page, etc.) and open the file **catalog/includes/footer.php**
2. Add a row to the footer table and insert your text, navigational links, or other edits to the footer.

Adding banner advertisements to the footer

You may also add advertisements from other companies or (even your for own products) to the footer. See the detailed chapter on Website Housekeeping.

Chapter

9

Other Customization

Save this chapter until you are familiar with and comfortable editing a line of code.

In this chapter:

Infobox headers, text in Infoboxes, and greetings can all be edited by web developers or store owners who use an HTML editor such as DreamWeaver or Front Page. If you have any difficulty, contact your installer.

Level of difficulty: medium.

Welcome, Guest! Would you like to edit your page titles or personal greeting? Or would you like to edit your Information Box headers or text? Then this chapter is for you.

TIP: Use "Search" or "Find" to locate the exact text you want to edit.

Changing the Page Title Text:

Open file includes/languages/english.php and

Search for this line	'TITLE'
Change only the text shown in **bold:**	define('TITLE', **'osCommerce'**);

Editing Personal Greetings:

To change the greeting, "Welcome, Guest! Would you like to log yourself in? Or would you prefer to create an account?"

Open file includes/languages/english.php and

Search for this line	'TEXT_GREETING_GUEST'
Change only the text shown in **bold:**	define('TEXT_GREETING_GUEST', **'Welcome** <span class="greetUser">**Guest!**</span> **Would you like to** <a href="%s"><u>**log yourself in**</u></a>**? Or would you prefer to** <a href="%s"><u>**create an account**</u></a>?');

To change the Personal Greeting, "Welcome back, username! Would you like to see which products are available to purchase?"

Open file includes/languages/english.php and

Search for this line	'TEXT_GREETING_PERSONAL'
Change only the text shown in **bold:**	define('TEXT_GREETING_PERSONAL', **'Welcome back** <span class="greetUser">%s!</span> **Would you like to see which** <a href="%s"><u>**new products**</u></a> **are available to purchase?'**);

To change the Personal Greeting, "If you are not username, please log yourself in with your account information"

Open file includes/languages/english.php and

Search for this line	'TEXT_GREETING_PERSONAL_RELOGON'
Change only the text shown in **bold:**	define('TEXT_GREETING_PERSONAL_RELOGON', '<small>If you are not %s, please <a href="%s"><u>log yourself in</u></a> with your account information.</small>');

To change the Personal Greeting, "Let's See What We Have Here":

Open file includes/languages/english.php and

Search for this line	'HEADING_TITLE'
Change only the text shown in **bold:**	define('HEADING_TITLE', **'Let\'s See What We Have Here'**);

Changing the Header Box Text on InfoBoxes

Quick Find

Figure 26
Infobox Header Text

Changing the Header Text on the Categories Box:

Open file includes/languages/english.php and

Search for this line	'BOX_HEADING_CATEGORIES'

Change only the text shown in **bold:**	define('BOX_HEADING_CATEGORIES', **'Categories'**);

Changing the Header Text on the Manufacturers Info Box:

Open file includes/languages/english.php and

Search for this line	'BOX_HEADING_MANUFACTURERS'
Change only the text shown in **bold:**	define('BOX_HEADING_MANUFACTURERS', **'Manufacturers'**);

Changing the Header Text on the What's New? Info Box:

Open file includes/languages/english.php and

Search for this line	'BOX_HEADING_WHATS_NEW'
Change only the text shown in **bold:**	define(**'BOX_HEADING_WHATS_NEW'**, **'What\'s New?'**);

Changing the Header Text on the Quick Find Info Box:

Open file includes/languages/english.php and

Search for this line	'BOX_HEADING_SEARCH'
Change only the text shown in **bold:**	define('BOX_HEADING_SEARCH', **'Quick Find'**);

Changing the Text within the Quick Find Info Box:

Open file includes/languages/english.php and

Search for this line	'BOX_SEARCH _TEXT'
Change only the text shown in **bold:**	define('BOX_SEARCH_TEXT', '**Use keywords to find the product you are looking for.**');

Changing the Advanced Search Text within the Quick Find Info Box:

Open file includes/languages/english.php and

Search for this line	' BOX_SEARCH_ADVANCED_SEARCH '
Change only the text shown in **bold:**	define('BOX_SEARCH_ADVANCED_SEARCH', '**Advanced Search**');

Changing the Header Text on the Specials Info Box:

Open file includes/languages/english.php and

Search for this line	'BOX_HEADING_SPECIALS'
Change only the text shown in **bold:**	define('BOX_HEADING_SPECIALS', '**Specials**');

Changing the Header Text on the Reviews Box:

Open file includes/languages/english.php and

Search for this line	'BOX_HEADING_REVIEWS'
Change only the text shown in **bold:**	define('BOX_HEADING_REVIEWS', '**Reviews**');

Changing the Text, "Write a review on this product" in the Reviews Box:

Open file includes/languages/english.php and

Search for this line	'BOX_REVIEWS _WRITE_REVIEW'
Change only the text shown in **bold:**	define('BOX_REVIEWS_WRITE_REVIEW', '**Write a review on this product!**');

Changing the Text, "There are currently no product reviews" in the Reviews Box:

Open file includes/languages/english.php and

Search for this line	' BOX_REVIEWS_NO_REVIEWS'
Change only the text shown in **bold:**	define('BOX_REVIEWS_NO_REVIEWS', '**There are currently no product reviews**');

Changing the Text, "# of 5 Stars!" in the Reviews Box:

Open file includes/languages/english.php and

Search for this line	' BOX_REVIEWS_TEXT_OF_5_STARS'
Change only the text shown in **bold:**	define('BOX_REVIEWS_TEXT_OF_5_STARS', '**%s of 5 Stars!**');

Changing the Header Text on the Shopping Cart Info Box:

Open file includes/languages/english.php and

Search for this line	' BOX_HEADING_SHOPPING_CART'
Change only the text	

shown in **bold:**	define('BOX_HEADING_SHOPPING_CART', **'Shopping Cart'**);

Changing the Text inside the Shopping Cart Info Box:

Open file includes/languages/english.php and

Search for this line	' BOX_SHOPPING_CART_EMPTY'
Change only the text shown in **bold:**	define('BOX_SHOPPING_CART_EMPTY', **'0 items'**);

Changing the Header Text on the Order History Info Box:

Open file includes/languages/english.php and

Search for this line	' BOX_HEADING_CUSTOMER_ORDERS'
Change only the text shown in **bold:**	define('BOX_HEADING_CUSTOMER_ORDERS', **'Order History'**);

Changing the Header Text on the Bestsellers Info Box:

Open file includes/languages/english.php and

Search for this line	' BOX_HEADING_BESTSELLERS'
Change only the text shown in **bold:**	define('BOX_HEADING_BESTSELLERS', **'Bestsellers'**);

Changing the Header Text on the Products Notifications Info Box:

Open file includes/languages/english.php and

Search for this line	' BOX_HEADING_NOTIFICATIONS'
Change only the text shown in **bold**:	define('BOX_HEADING_NOTIFICATIONS', **'Notifications'**);

Changing the "Notify me" Text in the Products Notifications Info Box:

Open file includes/languages/english.php and

Search for this line	' BOX_NOTIFICATIONS_NOTIFY'
Change only the text shown in **bold**:	define('BOX_NOTIFICATIONS_NOTIFY', **'Notify me of updates to %s'**);

Changing the "Do not notify me" Text in the Products Notifications Info Box:

Open file includes/languages/english.php and

Search for this line	' BOX_NOTIFICATIONS_NOTIFY_REMOVE'
Change only the text shown in **bold**:	define('BOX_NOTIFICATIONS_NOTIFY_REMOVE', **'Do not notify me of updates to %s'**);

Changing the Header Text on the Manufacturer Info Info Box:

Open file includes/languages/english.php and

Search for this line	' BOX_HEADING_MANUFACTURER_INFO '
Change only the text shown in **bold**:	define('BOX_HEADING_MANUFACTURER_INFO', **'Manufacturer Info'**);

Changing the "Manufacturers Homepage" Text in the Manufacturer Info Info Box:

Open file includes/languages/english.php and

Search for this line	'BOX_MANUFACTURER_INFO_HOMEPAGE'
Change only the text shown in **bold**:	define('BOX_MANUFACTURER_INFO_HOMEPAGE', '**%s Homepage**');

Changing the "Other Products" Text in the Manufacturer Info Info Box:

Open file includes/languages/english.php and

Search for this line	' BOX_MANUFACTURER_INFO_OTHER_PRODUCTS '
Change only the text shown in **bold**:	define('BOX_MANUFACTURER_INFO_OTHER_PRODUCTS', '**Other products**');

Changing the Header Text on the Languages Info Box:

Open file includes/languages/english.php and

Search for this line	'BOX_HEADING_SPECIALS'
Change only the text shown in **bold**:	define('BOX_HEADING_LANGUAGES', '**Languages**');

Changing the Header Text on the Currencies Info Box:

Open file includes/languages/english.php and

Search for this line	'BOX_HEADING_CURRENCIES'

Change only the text shown in **bold:**	define('BOX_HEADING_CURRENCIES', '**Currencies**');

Changing the Header Text on the Information Info Box:

Open file includes/languages/english.php and

Search for this line	'BOX_HEADING_INFORMATION'
Change only the text shown in **bold:**	define('BOX_HEADING_INFORMATION', '**Information**');

Changing the "Privacy Notice" Text in the Information Info Box:

Open file includes/languages/english.php and

Search for this line	'BOX_INFORMATION_PRIVACY'
Change only the text shown in **bold:**	define('BOX_INFORMATION_PRIVACY', '**Privacy Notice**');

Changing the "Conditions of Use" Text in the Information Info Box:

Open file includes/languages/english.php and

Search for this line	'BOX_INFORMATION_CONDITIONS'
Change only the text shown in **bold:**	define('BOX_INFORMATION_CONDITIONS', '**Conditions of Use**');

Changing the "Shipping & Returns" Text in the Information Info Box:

Open file includes/languages/english.php and

Search for this line	'BOX_INFORMATION_SHIPPING'
Change only the text shown in **bold**:	define('BOX_INFORMATION_SHIPPING', **'Shipping & Returns'**);

Changing the "Contact Us" Text in the Information Info Box:

Open file includes/languages/english.php and

Search for this line	'BOX_INFORMATION_CONTACT'
Change only the text shown in **bold**:	define('BOX_INFORMATION_CONTACT', **'Contact Us'**);

Changing the Header Text on the Tell A Friend Box:

Open file includes/languages/english.php and

Search for this line	'BOX_HEADING_TELL_A_FRIEND'
Change only the text shown in **bold**:	define('BOX_HEADING_TELL_A_FRIEND', **'Tell A Friend'**);

Changing the "Tell someone you know" Text in the Tell A Friend Box:

Open file includes/languages/english.php and

Search for this line	'BOX_TELL_A_FRIEND_TEXT'
Change only the text shown in **bold**:	define('BOX_TELL_A_FRIEND_TEXT', **'Tell someone you know about this product.'**);

Changing the Header Text on the Delivery Information Checkout Bar:

Open file includes/languages/english.php and

Search for this line	'CHECKOUT_BAR_DELIVERY'
Change only the text shown in **bold:**	define('CHECKOUT_BAR_DELIVERY', '**Delivery Information**');

Changing the Header Text on the Payment Information Checkout Bar:

Open file includes/languages/english.php and

Search for this line	'CHECKOUT_BAR_PAYMENT'
Change only the text shown in **bold:**	define('CHECKOUT_BAR_PAYMENT', '**Payment Information**');

Changing the Header Text on the Confirmation Checkout Bar:

Open file includes/languages/english.php and

Search for this line	'CHECKOUT_BAR_PAYMENT'
Change only the text shown in **bold:**	define('CHECKOUT_BAR_CONFIRMATION', '**Confirmation**');

Changing the Header Text on the Checkout Finished Checkout Bar:

Open file includes/languages/english.php and

Search for this line	'CHECKOUT_BAR_FINISHED'
Change only the text shown in **bold:**	define('CHECKOUT_BAR_FINISHED', '**Finished!**');

Chapter

10

Detailed Configuration

In this chapter:

In this chapter we examine each item in the **Configuration menu** in detail.

Level of difficulty: easy.

The detailed **Configuration menu** is where you tell your store its new name, your name, email address, set parameters and other details that will be used in many areas throughout the program.

To get to the **Configuration Menu** from the **Main Administration Menu**, click **Configuration:**

Configuration
My Store, Logging, Cache

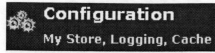

Figure 27
The Administrative Module's
Configuration Section

This brings you to the **Configuration menu** in the left-hand column:

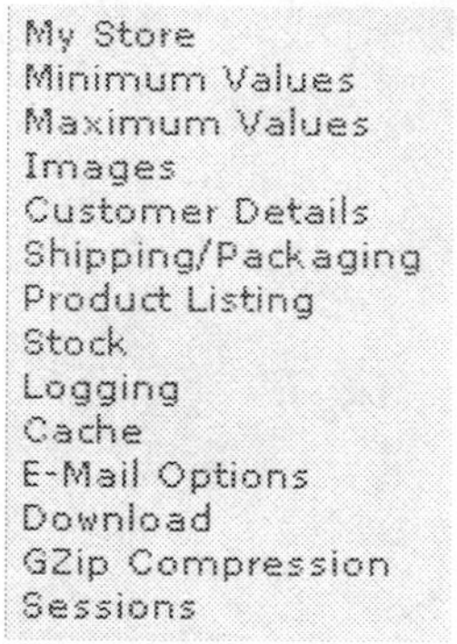
My Store
Minimum Values
Maximum Values
Images
Customer Details
Shipping/Packaging
Product Listing
Stock
Logging
Cache
E-Mail Options
Download
GZip Compression
Sessions

Figure 27
Left-Hand Configuration Menu

We will run through each item in the Configuration Menu in order, beginning with **My Store**.

My Store

Much of My Store was also covered in the Quick Start chapter. We add full explanation here of each item in My Store:

Title	
Store Name	Your Store's Name.
Store Owner	Your Name or your store name. This will appear in the purchase email that goes to your customers.
E-Mail Address	Your Email address for purchase email.
E-Mail From	When you send emails, the "From" address, usually yours.
Country	Your country, for shipping/tax purposes.
Zone	For shipping/tax purposes.
Expected Sort Order	Sort order in the expected products box.
Expected Sort Field	Column to sort by in expected products box.
Switch To Default Language Currency	So currency changes when language changed.
Send Extra Order Emails To	If you want to receive an email notifying you each time an order is placed.
Use Search-Engine Safe URLs (still in development)	This feature is not live yet.
Display Cart After Adding Product	If false, customer must click "shopping cart" in top right to view cart. If true, must click "continue" to return to products.
Allow Guest To Tell A Friend	Shows/hides "Tell A Friend" Infobox.
Default Search Operator	Select "and" or "or for visitors to search your products.
Store Address and Phone	Your Store's Address and Phone if you use check/money order module.
Show Category Counts	"True" shows # of products in category. "False" hides it.
Tax Decimal Places	Adds zeros to the pricing, i.e $1.00.
Display Prices with Tax	"True" adds tax to price. "False" does not.

Figure 28
The Configuration Menu's
My Store Module

Minimum Values

This is the minimum size of any field that will be filled in by the customer. If the customer tries to skip the field and not fill it in with these minimum values, they will receive an error message.

These are the minimum values of any field filled out by the customer. Don't change them unless you have a specific reason for doing so.

The DEFAULT values, or the minimum field size that is pre-set by the program when it is first installed, are shown in the "Value" column:

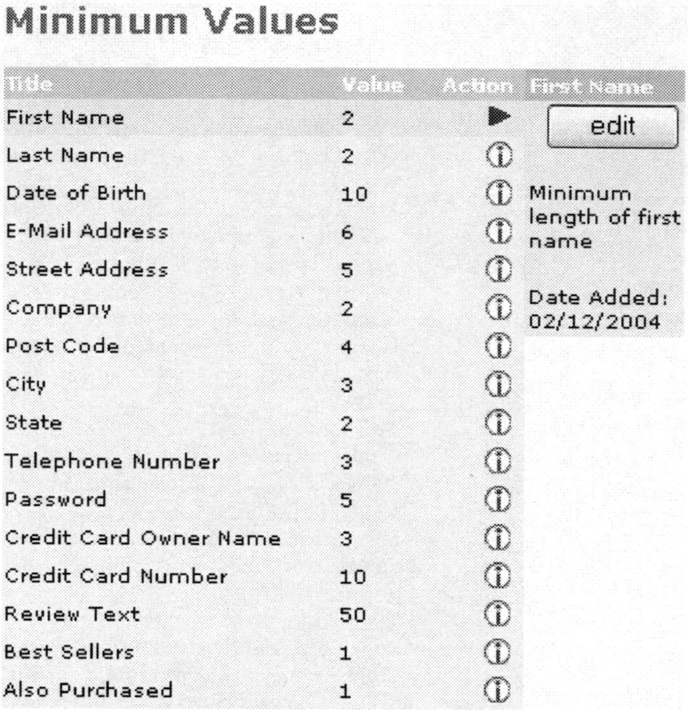

Minimum Values

Title	Value	Action	First Name
First Name	2	▶	edit
Last Name	2	ⓘ	
Date of Birth	10	ⓘ	Minimum length of first name
E-Mail Address	6	ⓘ	
Street Address	5	ⓘ	
Company	2	ⓘ	Date Added: 02/12/2004
Post Code	4	ⓘ	
City	3	ⓘ	
State	2	ⓘ	
Telephone Number	3	ⓘ	
Password	5	ⓘ	
Credit Card Owner Name	3	ⓘ	
Credit Card Number	10	ⓘ	
Review Text	50	ⓘ	
Best Sellers	1	ⓘ	
Also Purchased	1	ⓘ	

Figure 29
The Configuration Menu's
Minimum Values Module

Maximum Values

This is the maximum size of things that will affect the look and layout of your store. Again, unless you have a specific reason for changing them, it is best to leave them the way they are.

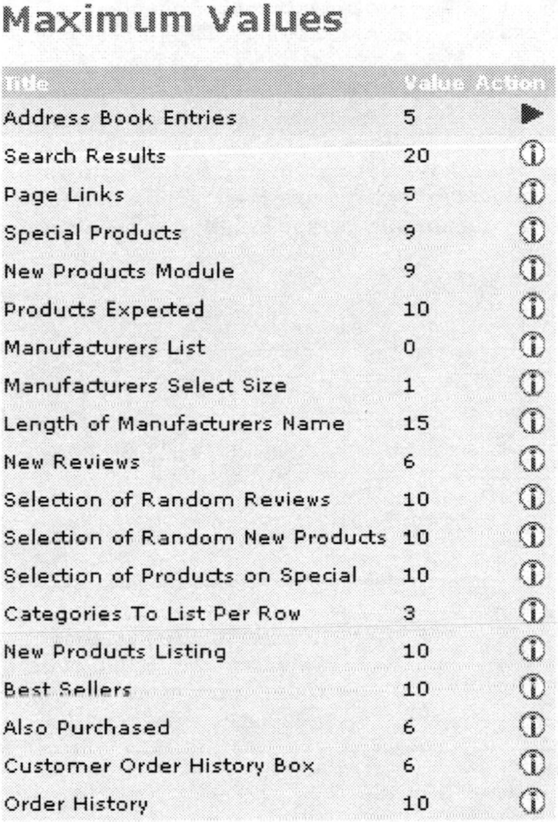

Maximum Values

Title	Value	Action
Address Book Entries	5	▶
Search Results	20	ⓘ
Page Links	5	ⓘ
Special Products	9	ⓘ
New Products Module	9	ⓘ
Products Expected	10	ⓘ
Manufacturers List	0	ⓘ
Manufacturers Select Size	1	ⓘ
Length of Manufacturers Name	15	ⓘ
New Reviews	6	ⓘ
Selection of Random Reviews	10	ⓘ
Selection of Random New Products	10	ⓘ
Selection of Products on Special	10	ⓘ
Categories To List Per Row	3	ⓘ
New Products Listing	10	ⓘ
Best Sellers	10	ⓘ
Also Purchased	6	ⓘ
Customer Order History Box	6	ⓘ
Order History	10	ⓘ

Maximum number of address book entries

How many products will be listed on each page.

How many page numbers at the bottom of your product listing.

How many specials in Specials entry

How many products in New Products entry

How many new products expected entry

How many manufacturers on mfrs' InfoBox.

How large Select box is on Mfrs page.

How long Manufacturers' names can be.

How many New Reviews to list.

How many Random review to list.

How many New Products in New Products box

How many random new products to list.

How many specials to list.

How many categories to list in each row.

How many new products to list.

How many best sellers to list.

How many products also purchased to list.

How many prior customer orders to list in customer history module.

How many orders to list in order module.

Figure 30
The Configuration Menu's
Maximum Values Module

Images

This is the size of the images you will upload for your store. Upload full size images, and osCommerce will reduce the images when they display on the products pages. This way customers can click the images to enlarge to full size.

 TIP: osCommerce comes with the image width set at 100 and the height at 80. Images look much better set at the *reverse* - width at 80 and height at 100. Likewise, Heading Image Width and Height can be reversed for a much more pleasing effect. Heading Image and Subcategory Image heights and widths are also reversed as of this writing.

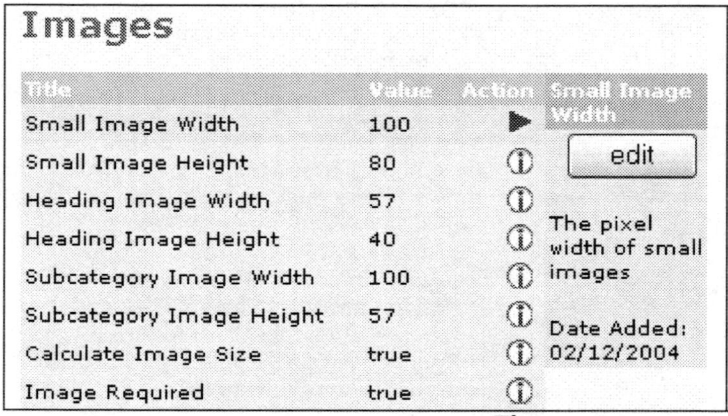

Images

Title	Value	Action
Small Image Width	100	▶
Small Image Height	80	ⓘ
Heading Image Width	57	ⓘ
Heading Image Height	40	ⓘ
Subcategory Image Width	100	ⓘ
Subcategory Image Height	57	ⓘ
Calculate Image Size	true	ⓘ
Image Required	true	ⓘ

Small Image Width

[edit]

The pixel width of small images

Date Added: 02/12/2004

Product listing page image width and height.
The image sizes that are uploaded for each category.

Sub-category image sizes.

If "False" then osCommerce will accept the default size. "False" if you do not want to use images.

**Figure 31
The Configuration Menu's
Images Module**

Customer Details

This is optional information that customers are required to reveal during the registration process. If you request irrelevant information, you may lose customers half-way through registration. Default values are set to "True."

Customer Details

Title	Value	Action	Gender
Gender	true	▶	edit
Date of Birth	true	ⓘ	
Company	true	ⓘ Display	
Suburb	true	ⓘ gender in th‹ customers	
State	true	ⓘ account	

Set to true if your product is gender-specific.
Set to true if you will personalize a product with a birthdate.
Set to true for business sales.
No idea why you would ask this.
State is calculated from zip, but you may use this as a check digit.

Figure 32
The Configuration Menu's
Customer Details Module

Shipping/Packaging

This is information needed for shipping calculations.

Shipping/Packaging

Title	Value	Action	Country of Origin
Country of Origin	United States	▶	edit
Postal Code	NONE	ⓘ	
Enter the Maximum Package Weight you will ship	50	ⓘ Select the country of origin to be	
Package Tare weight.	3	ⓘ used in shipping	
Larger packages - percentage increase.	10	ⓘ quotes.	

Set to the country you are shipping from.
Enter your postal or zip code.

Enter the maximum package weight your shipper will accept if you use "Ship by weight" Module.
Weight of typical packaging of small to medium packages
For 10% enter 10

Figure 33
The Configuration Menu's
Shipping/Packaging Module

Product Listing

This determines the order in which the product information is displayed on the products page. The first item to be displayed is 1, the second item to be displayed is 2, and so forth. Items you do not wish to display are left as zeros. NOTE: if you set more than one item to the same number, only one of them will display.

Product Listing

Title	Value	Action	
Display Product Image	1	▶	Display Product Image
Display Product Manufaturer Name	0	ⓘ	edit
Display Product Model	0	ⓘ	
Display Product Name	2	ⓘ	Do you want to display the Product Image?
Display Product Price	3	ⓘ	
Display Product Quantity	0	ⓘ	
Display Product Weight	0	ⓘ	Date Added: 02/12/2004
Display Buy Now column	4	ⓘ	
Display Category/Manufacturer Filter (0=disable; 1=enable)	1	ⓘ	
Location of Prev/Next Navigation Bar (1-top, 2-bottom, 3-both)	2	ⓘ	

See explanation above, the number in the Value column determines the order in which the item is displayed on the products page. Zero indicates this item will not be displayed on the page.

Category/Manufacturer Filter 1 means yes, 0 means no. If you want Prev/Next to display on both top and bottom, select 3, otherwise 1 for top only, 2 for bottom only.

Figure 34
The Configuration Menu's
Product Listing Module

Stock

This is an inventory control module that allows you to manage your inventory and re-order levels. It can also prevent customers from ordering products that are marked out of stock, so be careful if you decide to use it or you might lose sales. If you don't want to use it, be sure to set "Check stock level" to false.

Stock

Title	Value	Action	
Check stock level	true	▶	Check stock level
Subtract stock	true	ⓘ	edit
Allow Checkout	true	ⓘ	
Mark product out of stock	***	ⓘ	Check to see if sufficent stock is available
Stock Re-order level	5	ⓘ	

Checks to see if stock is available before adding to customer's cart
Keeps a running tally of inventory levels after each purchase.
Allows customers to check out even if item is below Stock Re-order level.
Allows you to mark products out of stock.
Number of items in stock when you wish to re-order.

Date Added: 02/12/2004

Figure 35
The Configuration Menu's Stock Module

Logging

There is no reason for store owners or website administrators to change any of the logging features of your store. This feature allows advanced programmers to change the location where database logging information is stored.

Logging				
Title	**Value**		**Action**	**Store Pag**
Store Page Parse Time	false		▶	Time
				ed
Log Destination	/var/log/www/tep/page_parse_time.log	ⓘ		Store the
Log Date Format	%d/%m/%Y %H:%M:%S	ⓘ		takes to p page
Display The Page Parse Time	true	ⓘ		Date Add 02/12/20
Store Database Queries	false	ⓘ		

Store the time it takes the server to read the page.
Directory and filename of page parse time log
The date format
Display the page parse time (store page parse time must be enabled)
Store the database queries in the page parse time log (PHP4 only)

Figure 36
The Configuration Menu's
Logging Module

Cache

Caching allows frequently accessed pages and images to be stored in a temporary directory for quicker page loading. You should be an advanced programmer to use this feature as the permissions on the folder where the cache is to be stored need to be changed to allow read, write and execute from the folder. If your store runs slowly, your installer may change the cache settings so it appears to run faster.

Cache			
Title	**Value**	**Action**	**Use Cache**
Use Cache	false	▶	edit
Cache Directory	/tmp/	ⓘ	
			Use caching features
			Date Added: 02/12/2004

Set to false or true.
Select the directory where cache files are stored.

Figure 37
The Configuration Menu's Cache Module

Email Options

Allows you to change email options. You should be an advanced programmer to use this feature.

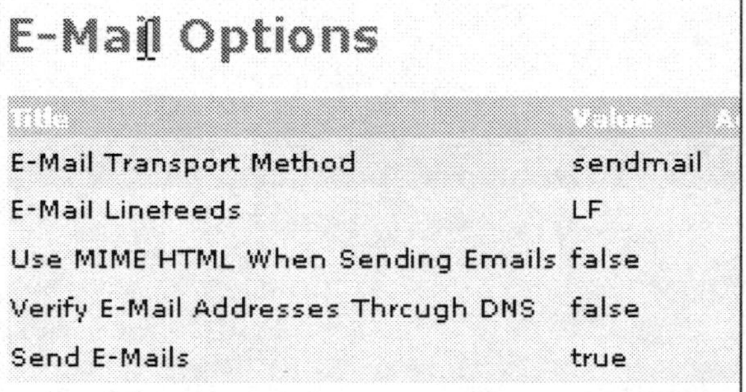 E-Mail Options		Defines if this server uses a local connection to sendmail or uses an SMTP connection via TCP/IP. Windows or MacOS servers should change this to SMTP.
Title	**Value**	
E-Mail Transport Method	sendmail	Defines the character sequence used to separate mail headers, LF or CRLF.
E-Mail Lineteeds	LF	Send e-mails in HTML format if set to true or plain text if set to false.
Use MIME HTML When Sending Emails	false	
Verify E-Mail Addresses Through DNS	false	Verify e-mail address through a DNS server or send unverified emails.
Send E-Mails	true	5. Send out e-mails or create without sending.

Figure 38
The Configuration Menu's
Email Options Module

Download

If you will be selling a product to be downloaded upon checkout, this feature needs to be set to true. You should be an advanced programmer to use this feature. **NOTE:** additional configuration needs to be done for this feature to be fully enabled. See explanation after Download menu table.

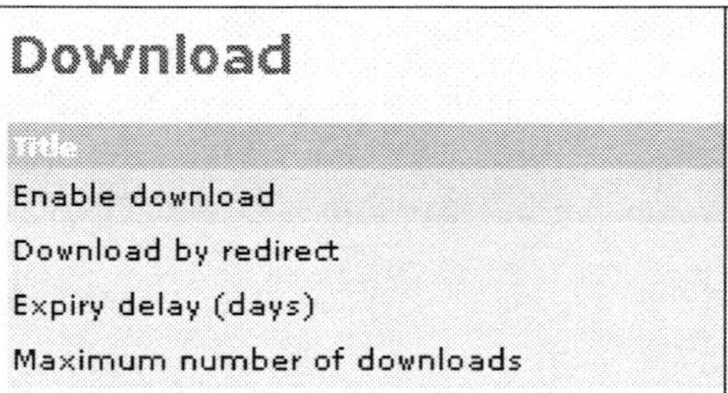

Download	
Title	
Enable download	Set to true if you wish to enable product downloads upon checkout.
Download by redirect	If you wish to use browser redirection for download. Disable on non-Unix systems.
Expiry delay (days)	Number of days before the download link expires. 0 means unlimited.
Maximum number of downloads	Total number of downloads authorized before customer link expires.

Figure 39
The Configuration Menu's
Download Module

 Additional Configuration is necessary for product download:

1. The product to be downloaded must be copied into the store's download folder: store/download/

2. The download will be read from the folder store/pub/, therefore, you or your installer need to set permissions for /store/pub to 777 and /store/download to 755.

3. Open file **/includes/configure.php** and add the following forward slash shown in **BOLD**:

Search for this line	'DIR_FS_DOWNLOAD',
Add the forward slash as shown in bold:	define('DIR_FS_DOWNLOAD', DIR_FS_CATALOG . 'download**/**');

4. Open file **/includes/configure.php** and add the following forward slash shown in **BOLD**:

Search for this line	'DIR_FS_DOWNLOAD_PUBLIC'
Add the forward slash as shown in bold:	define('DIR_FS_DOWNLOAD_PUBLIC', DIR_FS_CATALOG . 'pub**/**');

5. Using the **Administrative module**, go to **Administration, Catalog, Contents** and add the product information and images to the store. Note: Do not leave the product add/edit page, you need it for the next step.

6. If you have previously enabled download, you will see a new box displaying below the "Product Attributes" section where you can add the product as a download.

GZip Compression

GZip allows compression in your store pages for faster download of your store pages. Enabling GZip compression compresses the file that is sent to the web browser, where it is decompressed and rendered as normal. If the visitor's browser does not support compression, then a normal page is sent.

GZip Compression		
Title	**Value**	Enables HTTP GZip compression in your download of your store.
Enable GZip Compression	false	Use this compression level 0-9 (0 = minimum, 9 = maximum). If you have a lot of store traffic set compression to 9.
Compression Level	5	

Figure 40
The Configuration Menu's GZip Compression Module

Sessions

Sessions are topics for very advanced programmers. This sets security settings, cookies so the store can "remember' the customer as they move from one page to the next, and can allow or disallow known spiders (search engines) to search your website.

NOTE: If you set all your sessions settings to true, AOL users will not be able to use your store. Only "Force Cookie Use" and "Prevent Spider Sessions" can be used by AOL users.

Sessions	
Title	If sessions are file based, they are stored in this directory.
Session Directory	Force the use of sessions when cookies are only enabled.
Force Cookie Use	Validate the SSL_SESSION_ID on every secure HTTPS page request.
Check SSL Session ID	Validate the client's browser user agent on every page request.
Check User Agent	Validate the clients IP address on every page request.
Check IP Address	Prevent known spiders from starting a session.
Prevent Spider Sessions	Recreate the session to generate a new session ID when the customer logs on or creates an account (PHP >=4.1 needed).
Recreate Session	

Figure 41
The Configuration Menu's
Sessions Module

Chapter

11

Product Management

In this chapter:

We work our way through the Products, Categories, and Manufacturers section of the Catalog menu of the Administrative Module.

Level of difficulty: easy to medium, depending on the complexity of your products.

How to manage your products:

1. List your product categories.
2. List your product attributes (size, color, etc.).
3. List your manufacturer names and websites (optional).

4. Look at the sample categories and products included in the standard installation, then edit or delete them.
5. Now enter your products in their categories.

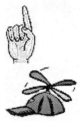

TIP: If you want to get started quickly entering individual products, turn to the Quick Start Guide at the beginning of this book.
Do you have dozens or hundreds of products and images to enter? If so, there are add-in products, or "contributions" such as EZPopulate that can add your products and images in one batch. These contributions can also delete all the example categories and products. Ask your installer to set it up for you or check the Appendix at the back of this book.

List your product categories

To begin managing your products, from the **main Administration menu**, click **Catalog.**

Catalog
Contents, Manufacturers

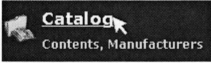

Figure 42
Main Administration Menu

This brings you to Catalog Categories/Products. Here is the full **Catalog menu** that you will find on the left of every page. We will examine each of these items in detail:

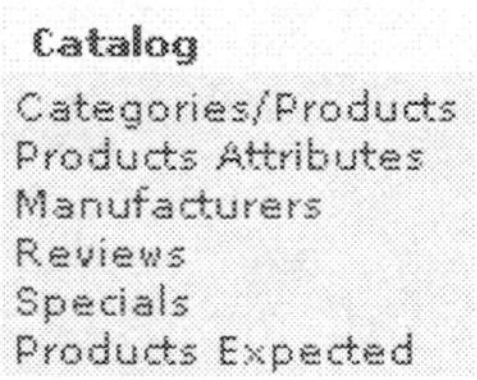

Catalog
Categories/Products
Products Attributes
Manufacturers
Reviews
Specials
Products Expected

Figure 43
The Administrative Module's Catalog Menu

Menu Item	Description
Categories/ Products	Enter the categories you want listed in the "Categories" infobox on your website, then enter basic product information about each of your products on this screen.

Products Attributes	Detailed information about each product.
Manufacturers	Optional. If you would like to enter a link to your manufacturers' websites, and an image of their logos, you may do so here.
Reviews*	Edit reviews that customers have left about your products.
Specials*	List products that are on special, their sale price or percentage price cut, and the automatic expiration date of the special.
Products Expected*	If you have listed products with an "expected" date, this screen allows you to edit them all without going into each individual product.

*These 3 menu items are covered in the **Website Housekeeping** chapter.

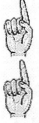

TIP: Each product MUST be put in a category (unless you only sell a handful of products). This means you need to *first* create the categories.

TIP: If you will want to display Manufacturers' names (with optional link to the manufacturers' sites), STOP HERE and add the manufacturers' names FIRST. The Manufacturers' box does NOT show up unless you have inserted manufacturers' names in them.

In **Categories/Products,** if you have not yet removed them in the Quick Start Guide chapter, there will 3 sample test categories to get you started:

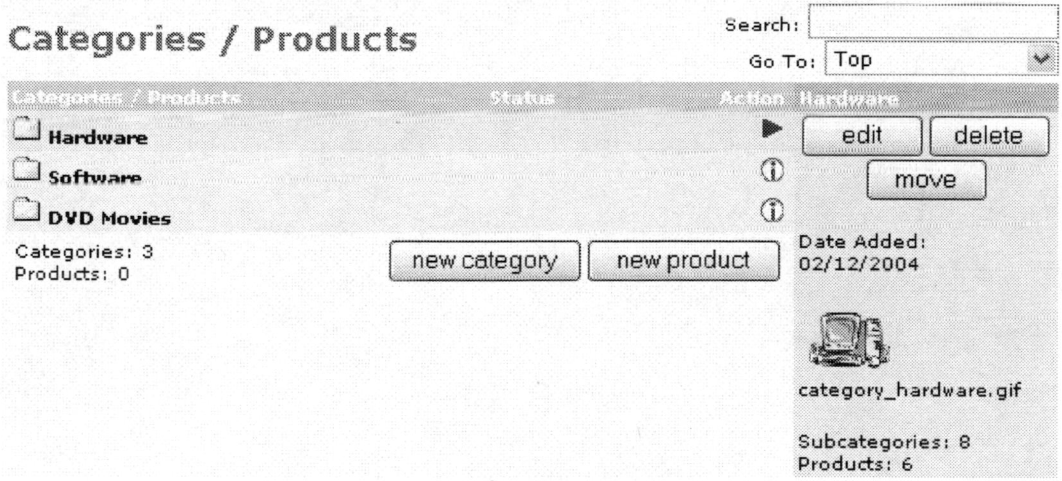

Categories / Products

Search: [   ]
Go To: Top ⌄

Categories / Products	Status	Action Hardware
📁 **Hardware**	▶	edit · delete
📁 **Software**	ⓘ	move
📁 **DVD Movies**	ⓘ	

Categories: 3
Products: 0

[new category] [new product]

Date Added: 02/12/2004

category_hardware.gif

Subcategories: 8
Products: 6

Figure 44
The Catalog Menu's
Categories/Products Menu

TIP: Click the sample test categories and select to see how they are set up, but be sure to DELETE the sample categories before your store goes live.

TIP: Enter ONE category, its product attributes, manufacturer, and product to test your site, THEN enter remaining products when you know you have done it properly.

Adding a Category:

Before you can add your own products, you must first create a **Category** for it.

Click the **New Category** button and fill in the appropriate information. If you want this category to be listed FIRST in your category listing, enter "1" in the Sort Order box:

New Category

Please fill out the following information for the new category

Category Name:

Category Image:

[Browse...]

Sort Order:

[save] [cancel]

Figure 45
The Catalog Section's
"New Category" Menu

2. List your product options

This section allows you to enter specific attributes that apply to your products, such as size and color.

If the product you are selling is software to be downloaded, and you have set up the download, you will see additional product options here. Turn to the Download section for more

information.

TIP: Drawing a chart that lists your product attributes makes it easier to enter this information. See sample below.

Option	Value	Price
Size	S M L XL	5.00 5.00 5.00 10.00
Color	Red Yellow Blue	

Figure 46
Sample Product Attributes Chart

TIP: It is much easier to work with one product option at a time, defining the option, value and attribute, before moving on to the next product option.

To begin entering your product options, select the **INSERT button** and enter the required information:

Product Options

Option ID ⌄

1 |

ID	Option Name	Action	
1	Color	edit	delete
2	Size	edit	delete
3	Model	edit	delete
4	Memory	edit	delete
5	Version	edit	delete
6	en: [ ]	insert	

Figure 47
The Catalog Menu's
Product Options Module

Option Values

Once you have set up your product options (size, color, etc.), next you will set up the "values" of each option:

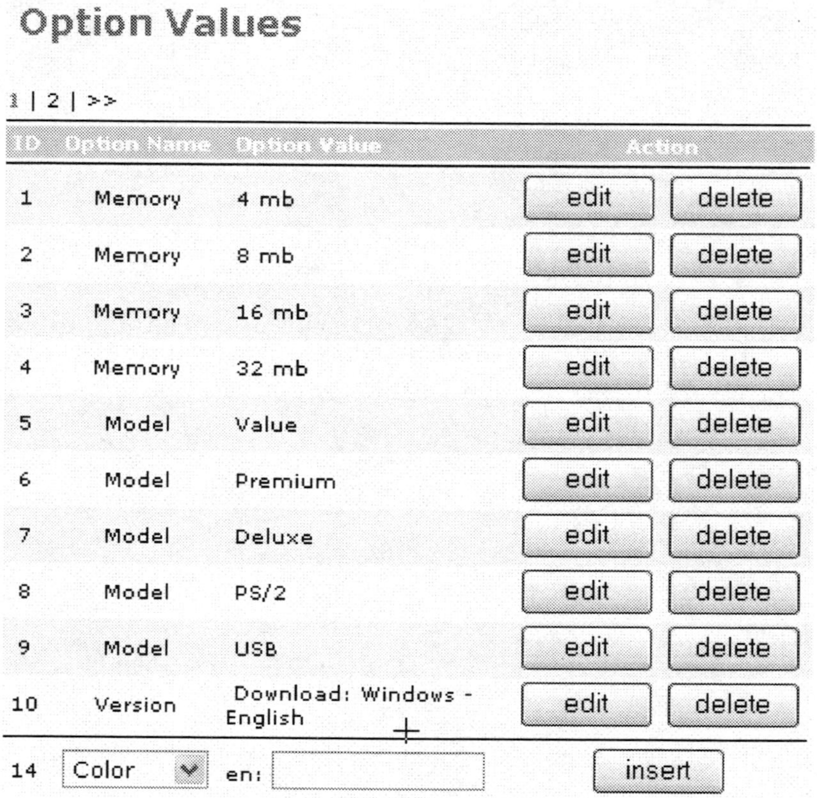

Option Values

1 | 2 | >>

ID	Option Name	Option Value	Action	
1	Memory	4 mb	edit	delete
2	Memory	8 mb	edit	delete
3	Memory	16 mb	edit	delete
4	Memory	32 mb	edit	delete
5	Model	Value	edit	delete
6	Model	Premium	edit	delete
7	Model	Deluxe	edit	delete
8	Model	PS/2	edit	delete
9	Model	USB	edit	delete
10	Version	Download: Windows - English	edit	delete
14	Color ▾	en:	insert	

Figure 48
The Catalog Menu's
Product Option Values Module

The product attributes that you listed in the Option values screen will also be listed in the Option Name column. For example, if you set up attributes for "Size" and "Colors" it will be listed on the Products Attributes screen in the Option Name column:

Products Attributes

1 | 2 | >>

ID	Product Name	Option Name	Option Value	Value Price	Prefix	Action
1	Matrox G200 MMS	Memory	4 mb	0.0000	+	edit delete
2	Matrox G200 MMS	Memory	8 mb	50.0000	+	edit delete
3	Matrox G200 MMS	Memory	16 mb	70.0000	+	edit delete
4	Matrox G200 MMS	Model	Value	0.0000	+	edit delete
	A Bug's Life ▾	Color ▾	16 mb ▾		+	insert

Figure 49
The Catalog Menu's
Products Attributes Module

TIP: If all your prices for a product are the same, skip to the next section.

Finally, under Products Attributes, the Value Price column allows you to specify different pricing for, say, X-Large clothing.

EXAMPLE:

To charge $5 for regular size clothing, and $10 for Extra-Large clothing, leave the value price as 0.00 for small, medium, and large clothing and change X-Large to $5 + to the regular price.

You can also charge LESS for an item. For example, let's say you charge half price for infant size.

EXAMPLE:

You charge $5 for regular size clothing, and only $2.50 for infant sized clothing, leave the value price as 0.00 for small, medium, and large clothing and change "Infant" size to $2.50 – (minus sign).

3. List your manufacturer names (optional)

If you would like to include manufacturers' names, logos and a link to their website, complete this section FIRST. It is a good idea to delete the manufacturers that are included as samples.

From the **main Administration menu**, click **Catalog**, then in the left column click **Manufacturers**.

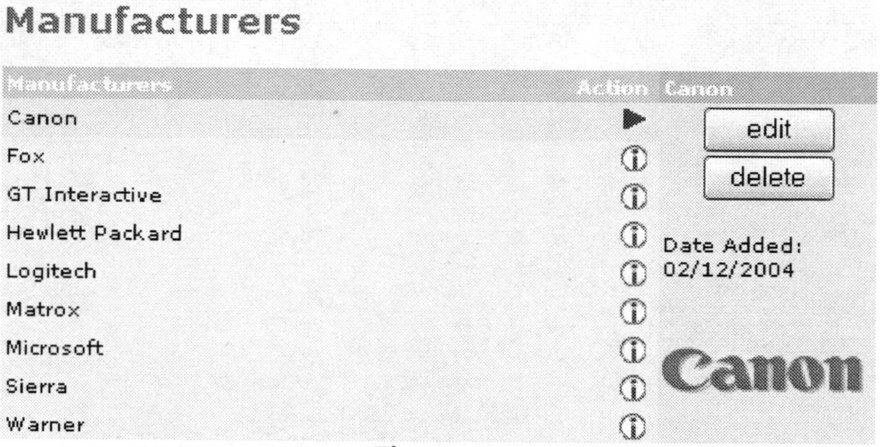

Manufacturers

Figure 50
Sample manufacturers included with standard installation
It is a good idea to delete them.

To Add or Edit a Manufacturer

Click Edit or Add, and insert the manufacturer's name, image from your computer, and the manufacturer's address (URL):

Figure 51
The Catalog Menu's
Add or Edit Manufacturer Module

4. Enter products

Adding a new product:

After you have added your categories, product attributes, and manufacturers (optional), SELECT the category by clicking the new category name. Here the Action category has been clicked:

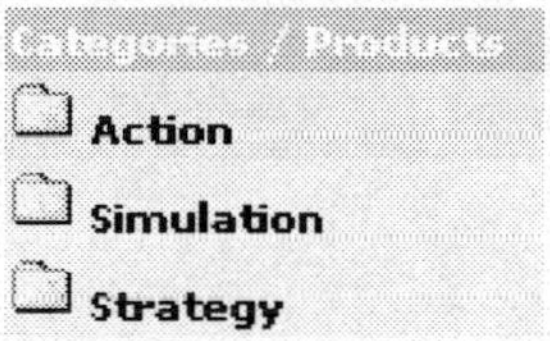

Categories / Products

☐ **Action**

☐ **Simulation**

☐ **Strategy**

Figure 52
The Catalog Menu's
Add Categories Module

Now you can add a new product to your new category.

IN THE APPROPRIATE CATEGORY, click the **New Category** button.

TIP: If the top of your new product page says "NEW PRODUCT IN TOP", then you forgot to select a Category name. Go back and click a Category name.

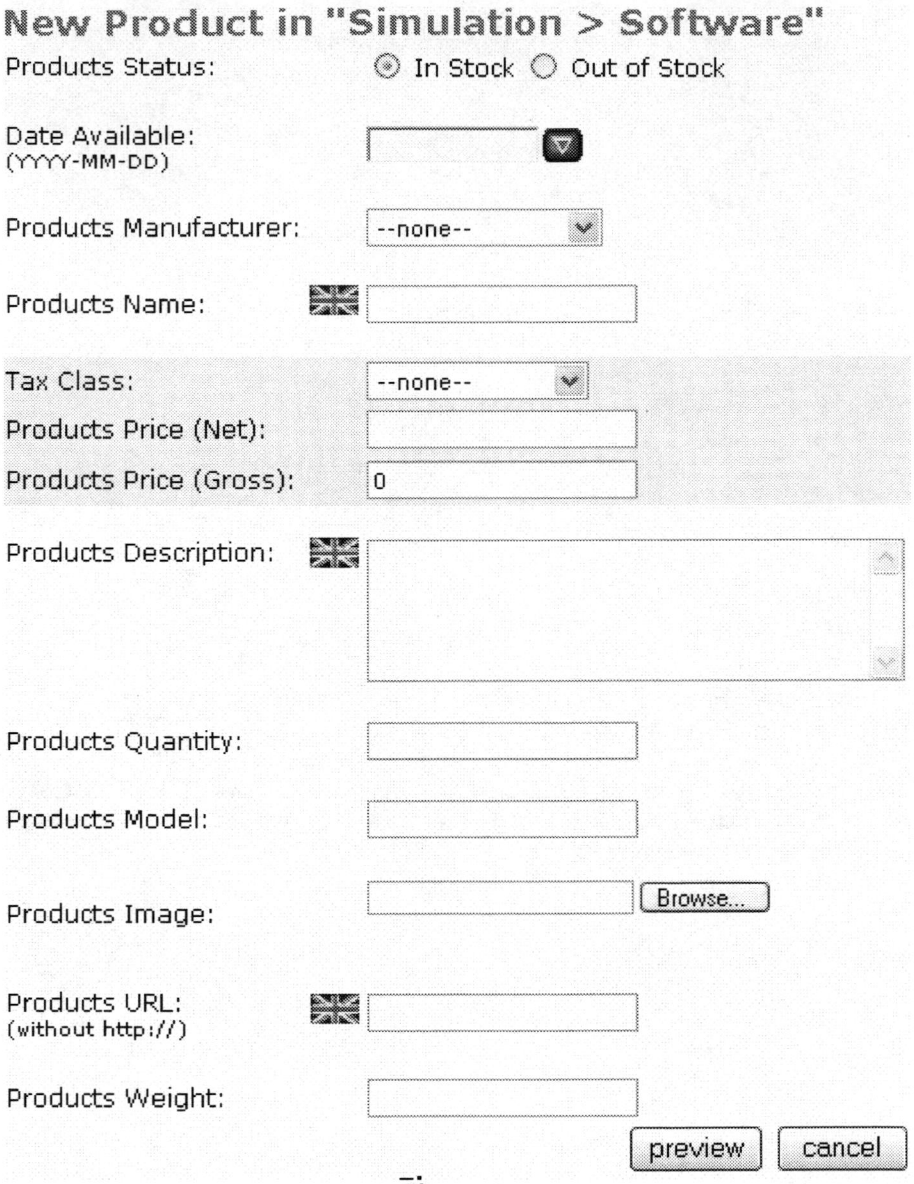

New Product in "Simulation > Software"

Products Status: ⊙ In Stock ○ Out of Stock

Date Available: [▼]
(YYYY-MM-DD)

Products Manufacturer: [--none--   ▼]

Products Name: 🇬🇧 [   ]

Tax Class: [--none--   ▼]
Products Price (Net):   [   ]
Products Price (Gross):   [0   ]

Products Description: 🇬🇧 [▲]
                             [   ]
                             [   ]
                             [▼]

Products Quantity: [   ]

Products Model: [   ]

Products Image: [   ] [Browse...]

Products URL: 🇬🇧 [   ]
(without http://)

Products Weight: [   ]

                          [preview] [cancel]

Figure 53
The Catalog Menu's New Product Entry Module
See next page for description of entries

Item	Description
Products Status	"In Stock" is selected. If you run out, return and click "Out of Stock."
Date Available	Leave blank for today's date unless it will be available in the future.
Products Manufacturer	If you have previously entered Manufacturers in the Admin Module's Catalog-Manufacturers screen, they will display here. Otherwise go back and add them now.
Products Name	The Product Name you wish to give it.
Tax Class	If you have previously entered Tax Class in the Admin Module's Locations/Taxes screen, they will display here. Otherwise go back and add them now.
Products Price (Net)	Enter the price that you want displayed in your store
Products Price (Gross)	Gross Price is automatically calculated so you can see the total price with tax if the item is marked as a taxable good.
Products Description	The description that the customer will see.
Products Quantity	How many you have in stock. This number will tick down as customers make purchases. It will read "Out of Stock" if this number reaches zero. You may choose to leave this blank.
Products Model	Your product's model name or number for your reference.
Products Image	Click the **BROWSE** button to select the image from your computer. NOTE: if it will not upload, contact your installer to set "write permissions" on the IMAGES directory.
Products URL	If you already have a separate web page with a detailed description of your product.
Products Weight	If you are using "weight" as a shipping module, you will need to list the weight of your item including its packaging. IF YOU FORGET TO ADD WEIGHT, SHIPPING COSTS WILL BE CALCULATED AT ZERO.

If your product is a download, be sure to set weight at zero, or flat rate shipping will be added to your downloads. |

Figure 54
New Product Detail

After you enter your first product, click the **PREVIEW button**, then the **SAVE button**.

Repeat for each of your products.

Chapter

12

Customer & Order Management

In this chapter:

"Customer Management" & "Order Management" are the daily operations reports you need to run your business. Customer management means maintaining the files about your customers. Order management means the actual orders from your customers. In this chapter we examine each in detail.

Level of difficulty: easy.

TIP: To view strategic, top-level management reports such as top sellers, top viewed products, and top customers, go to the Management Reports chapter.

To begin managing your products, from the **main Administration menu**, click **Customers.**

This brings you to the **left-hand Customers menu:**

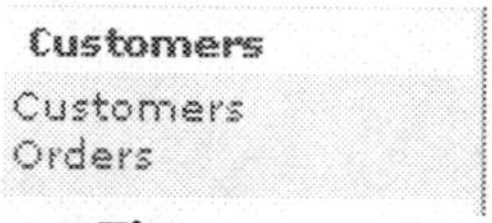

Figure 55
Customers Menu

Menu Item	Description
Customers	List of all your customers except for their passwords. You may edit their information (for example, if they change their address), delete them, or look at a list of all their orders to date.
Orders	List of your customers orders. You may edit, change the order status (ie to "shipped"), email the customer about their order status, or generate an invoice or packing slip.

Click **Customers** to see the **Customers screen.**

Customer Management

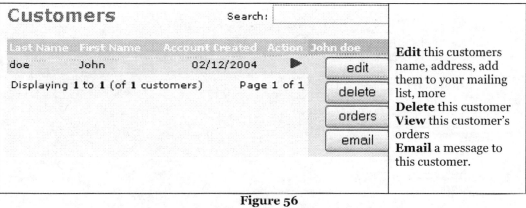

Figure 56
The Customers Menu's
Customer Management Module

To Edit a Customer's Record

You may need to do this if, for example, the customer has moved email addresses and can no longer access his forgotten password. Or perhaps they forgot that they signed up for your newsletter, and tell you they no longer wish to receive it.

From the **Customers** screen click the **EDIT** button.

Next Page: Figure 57, The Customers Menu's Edit Customer Module

Customers

Personal

Gender: ⦿ Male   ◯ Female

First Name: `John`   * Required

Last Name: `doe`   * Required

Date of Birth: `01/01/2001`   * Required

E-Mail Address: `root@localhost` * Required

Company

Company name: `ACME Inc.`

Address

Street
Address: `1 Way Street`   * Required

Suburb: `              `

Post Code: `12345`   * Required

City: `NeverNever`   * Required

State: `California`

Country: `United States` ▾

Contact

Telephone Number: `12345`   * Required

Fax Number: `              `

Options

Newsletter: `Unsubscribed` ▾

[update] [cancel]

To Delete a Customer's Record

From the **Customers** screen click the **DELETE** button. You will be asked to confirm the delete, simply select **DELETE** again.

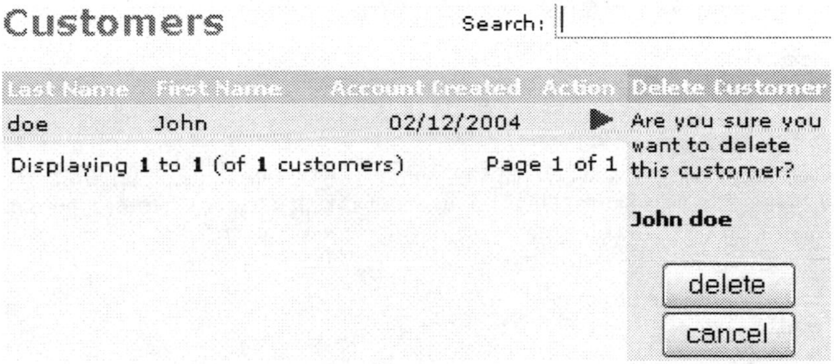

Customers   Search: |

Last Name	First Name	Account Created	Action	Delete Customer
doe	John	02/12/2004	▶	Are you sure you want to delete this customer?

Displaying 1 to 1 (of 1 customers)   Page 1 of 1

John doe

delete

cancel

Figure 58
The Customers Menu's
Delete Customer Module

To View or Print a Customer's Orders

This is very important! For good records management, you should print a copy of EACH order as it comes in. You should also perform a complete database backup weekly to complete your records management. See the Website Housekeeping chapter for more information on backups.

From the **Customers** screen click the **VIEW** button.

Click the **EDIT** button to see the order. You may also change the status of the order, print the order for your records, or put comments in the comments box.

Note that if the "Send Comments to Customer" box is checked, whatever you put in the Comments box will be sent as an email to the customer.

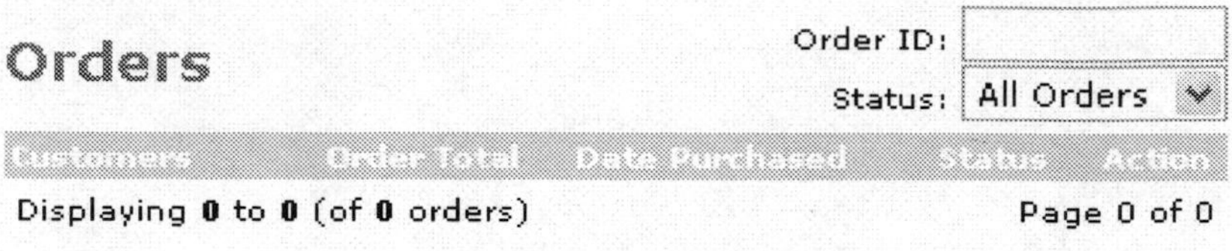

Orders

Order ID:

Status: All Orders ▼

Customers	Order Total	Date Purchased	Status	Action

Displaying **0** to **0** (of **0** orders)   Page 0 of 0

Figure 59
The Customers Menu's
View Customer Orders Module

To Send an Email to a Customer

From the **Customers** screen click the **EMAIL** button. NOTE that this is separate from the "Newsletter Management" section. This simply sends an email to the customer; perhaps notifying them of a delay in shipping, a color that is no longer carried, and so forth.

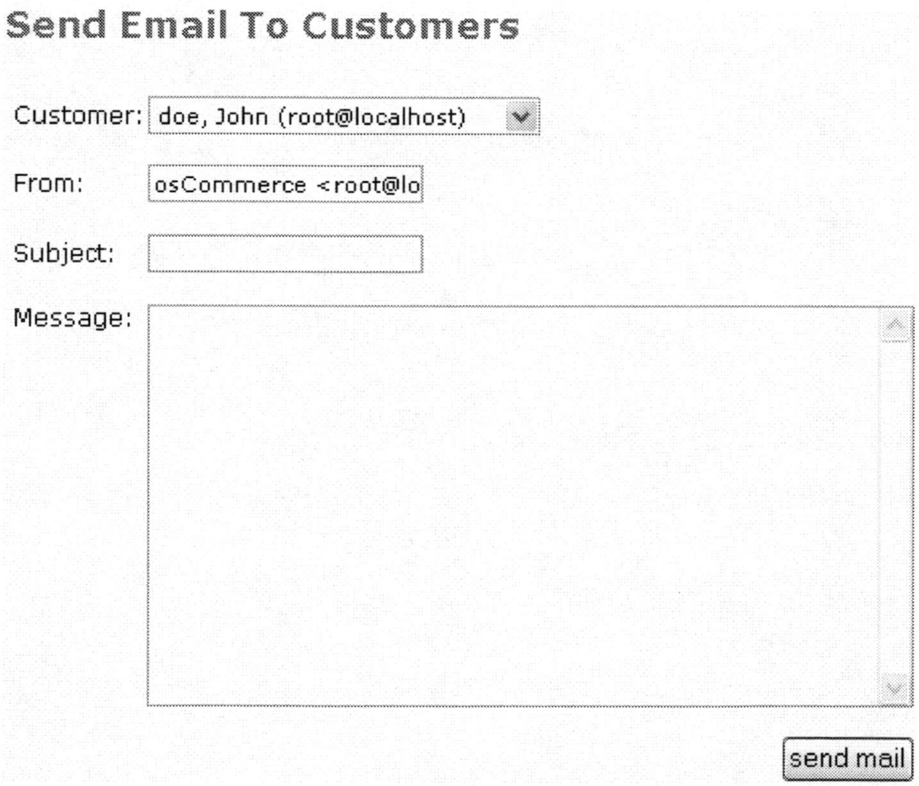

Send Email To Customers

Customer: doe, John (root@localhost) ▼

From: osCommerce <root@lo

Subject:

Message:

send mail

**Figure 60
The Customers Menu's
Send Email to Customer Module**

Order Management

To manage your orders, you will want to:

1. Sort pending orders.
2. Generate packing slips and package up your orders.
3. Generate an invoice (if you have not automatically received payment before the order was placed),
4. (optional) Send an email notifying the customer of shipping; and then
5. Change the order status to delivered.

To begin managing your orders, from the **main Administration menu**, click **Customers.**

This brings you to the **Customers menu.** Click on **Orders:**

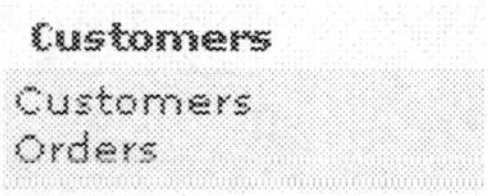

Customers
Customers
Orders

**Figure 61
Customer Orders Menu**

Menu Item	Description
Orders	List of your orders from customers, sorted by status: all orders, pending, processed, or delivered. You may edit, change the order status (ie to "shipped"), print, email the customer about their order status, or generate an invoice or packing slip.

1. Sort pending orders

To see pending orders, from the left-hand **Customers** menu, click **ORDERS** and change **Status** to **Pending**:

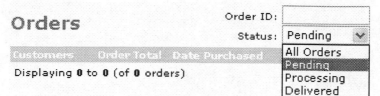

Figure 62
The Customers Menu's
Pending Orders Module

If you wish to print a complete list of pending orders, from your **browser's top navigation bar** select **FILE-PRINT**.

2. Generate packing slips and package up your orders

Generate your **packing slips** from the Pending orders screen by clicking the **PACKING SLIP** button, and package up your orders.

3. Generate an invoice

Generate your **invoices** from the Pending orders screen by clicking the **INVOICE** button, and include it with your order.

4. Send an email to the customer

Send an email to the customer notifying them of shipping.

5. Change the order status to delivered.

Once you have sent the package, From the Order screen, change the drop-down status box of each order to **DELIVERED**. NOTE: if you sent a separate email notifying them of shipping, be sure to un-check "SEND COPY TO CUSTOMER" or they will receive another email notifying them of the change in status.

6. Keep a paper copy of the order for your records.

In case you were to have a disaster such as (gasp) not being able to connect to the Internet, you should keep a paper copy of the order at least until your next regularly scheduled website backup. See the chapter on Website Housekeeping for more info. To print a copy of the customer's filled order, select **File- Print. Keep the paper copy in a safe place.**

Chapter

13

Management Reports

In this chapter:

Management Reports are strategic, top-level reports that the store owner or manager will enjoy seeing, which report on top sellers, top viewed products, and top customers.

Level of difficulty: easy.

TIP: These are top level reports. If you are looking for daily operations reports (i.e. orders pending, received, processed, etc.), go to the Customers Chapter.

Viewing Management Reports

To begin viewing management reports, from the **main Administration menu**, click **REPORTS.**

This brings you to the left-column **Reports Menu.**

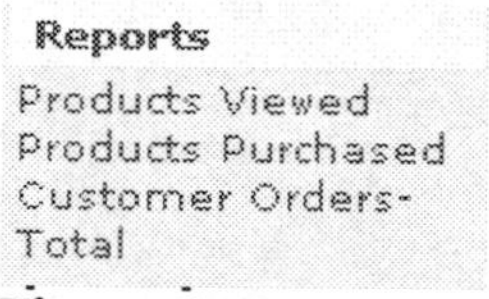

Reports
Products Viewed
Products Purchased
Customer Orders-
Total

Figure 63
Management Reports
Module

Reports Menu Item	Description
Products Viewed	Most popularly viewed products, from most to least viewed. Helps you track expected product popularity.
Products Purchased	Most popularly purchased products, from most to least viewed. Helps you track actual product popularity.
Customer Orders-Total	Which customers have purchased the most items, listed from most frequent buyers to least. Helps you track who to market to.

Sample Management Report

Best Viewed Products	
No. Products	Viewed
01. A Bug's Life (English)	9
02. Under Siege (English)	5
03. The Matrix (English)	1
04. Matrox G200 MMS (English)	0
05. Matrox G400 32MB (English)	0

Figure 64
The Reports Menu's
Best Viewed Products Module

To Print Management Reports

If you wish to print the **Best Viewed Products Report, Products Purchased Report** or **Customer Orders - Total Report**, from your browser's top navigation bar simply select **FILE-PRINT**.

Chapter

14

Payment and Order
Checkout

In this chapter:

In this chapter we link your store with your credit card processor, and specify the order in which the payment process takes place. This chapter covers the Modules menu Payment and Order sections.

Level of difficulty: easy to medium.

It is easy to enable sophisticated and secure payment schemes with osCommerce simply by signing up for an account with one of the pre-packaged credit card processors, and entering the account information they provide.

If you wish to manually process your own credit cards, you MUST put your store on a SECURE SERVER (https://) to protect the credit card numbers of your customers, or you will risk having the numbers stolen by computer hackers. CONTACT YOUR INSTALLER.

TIP: You must *first* open an account with one of the companies listed in order to process your payments through them. It may take several days to receive account information from them, so sign up as soon you have selected a processor.

TIP: If you don't see your credit card processor listed here, ask your installer to see if an add-on or "contribution" is available.

Selecting the Payment Processor Right for You

Getting information from these companies is like pulling teeth. If they want you to be their customer, why do they make it so difficult? Why must they obfuscate the very information you need?

I have researched as much information as I could about each company to come up with the following comparison table. This comparison answers the nitty-gritty questions that YOU care about:

1. What countries does it work in?
2. How much does it cost?
3. How long of a commitment is it? And
4. How easy or difficult is it to install?

Please see the detailed information about each company in the sections that follow. Once you have decided on a payment processor, follow the directions to apply for an account with them, and then continue this section.

	US	UK	EUR	CAN	AUS	OTHER	INITIAL FEE	MO.	TRANSACTION	TERM	SSL Req'd?	Ease of Setup*
Cash on Delivery	X	X	X	X	X	X			---		N	1
Check/ Money Order	X	X	X	X	X	X			---		N	1
Credit Card	X	X	X	X	X	X			---		Y	1
PayPal	X	X	X	X	X	X	0	0	2.9% + .30	1 Day	N	2
2CheckOut	X	X	X	X	X	X	49	0	5.5%	1 Day	Y	2
iPayment	X						0	25-35	2.25% + .30	30 Day	Y	3
Authorize. net	X						299	20	2.4% + .10	30 Day	Y	2
PsiGate	X			X			199	25	2.25% + .30 2.6%	1 Yr	Y	3
NO-CHEX		X					0	0	+20p		Y	3
SECPay		X					50£	10-20£	20p to 1.9%		Y	3
ESEC/Secu repay**					X		Flat $AU <6000		$1000 <3000 trans, $1500		Y	2
Paymate Express 2.0**					X		0	AU $0 to $33	1.7 to 2.4%		Y	2

*1=easy, 2=medium, 3=more difficult

**Payment Contributions must be installed separately.

Link your store to payments

To begin linking your store to your credit card processor or to activate your manual credit card process, from the main **Administration menu**, click **Modules**.

Figure 65
Main Administration Menu
Modules Section

This brings you to Payment Modules. This is a list of **third-party credit card processors** that can be automatically installed.

Payment Modules

Modules	Sort Order	
Authorize.net	0	Use your Authorize.net account
Credit Card	0	Manually process credit cards
Cash on Delivery	0	Accept CODs
iPayment		iPaymentinc.com
Check/Money Order	0	Accept checks or MO's by mail
NOCHEX		nochex.com
PayPal	0	PayPal.com
2CheckOut	0	2checkout.com
PSiGate		psigate.com
SECPay		secpay.com

Figure 66
The Module Menu's
Payment Modules Menu

To install a payment module, simply click the **Install button**.

NOTE: I have reviewed 3 additional modules which need to be installed as separate "contributions" by your installer. Two are for Australians: ESEC/Securepay and PayMate, and Linkpoint which is a worldwide processor.

TIP: The third-party credit-card processors use secure servers, so you may not have to. Check with them to be certain.

TIP: Install only ONE payment module at a time, then thoroughly test your site to make sure it is working properly. Only then should you proceed to add another if you wish.

After you have installed a processor, you can then edit it. Highlight the processor you wish to edit by clicking the "i" symbol in the Action Column and click the **EDIT button,** then the **INSTALL button**.

Authorize.Net

Authorize.net is one of the most respected US credit card processors. Their system is easy to set up and install. You can get an account with them through one of their resellers in 24-48 hours. Their Resellers will answer any questions you have and walk you through installation. See http://www.authorizenet.com/reseller/directory.php

NEXT PAGE: Figure 67 Authorize.net install menu

Authorize.net

Enable Authorize.net Module
Do you want to accept Authorize.net paymer

To begin using Authorize.net, you must select TRUE.

⊙ True

○ False

Login Username
The login username used for the Authorize.r
service

Enter the login username provided by Authorize.net.

testing

Transaction Key
Transaction Key used for encrypting TP data

Enter the transaction key provided by Authorize.net.

Test

Transaction Mode
Transaction mode used for processing order

While you are testing, select TEST. This ensures the credit card numbers you enter will not be charged. YOU MUST CHANGE THIS TO PRODUCTION WHEN YOUR STORE IS LAUNCHED.

⊙ Test

○ Production

Transaction Method
Transaction method used for processing ord

Select the transaction method you specified to Authorize.net.

⊙ Credit Card

○ eCheck

Customer Notifications
Should Authorize.Net e-mail a receipt to the
customer?

If you wish Authorize.net to email a receipt to the customer, select TRUE. If you will manually email receipts, select FALSE.

○ True

⊙ False

Payment Zone
If a zone is selected, only enable this paym
method for that zone.

You can accept, say, checks or cash only in certain zones that you have established in the LOCATIONS/TAXES menu.

--none-- ▾

Orders can be automatically set to "PENDING, PROCESSING or DELIVERED."

Set Order Status
Set the status of orders made with this payn
module to this value

You can enable multiple methods of payment; the sort order is a column on the PAYMENT MODULES screen. Zero will be displayed first, 1 next, etc.

default ▾

Sort order of display.
Sort order of display. Lowest is displayed firs

Click the **Update button** when finished.

0

[update] [cancel]

Credit Cards

Select Credit Card if you wish to manually process your own credit cards. For example, if you are a retailer who manually swipes your customer's cards.

 If you use this module, you MUST put your store on a Secure Server to protect the credit card numbers of your customers, or you will risk having the numbers stolen by computer hackers. CONTACT YOUR INSTALLER.

Credit Card

Enable Credit Card Module
Do you want to accept credit card payments?

◉ True

○ False

You must select TRUE for this module to work.

Split Credit Card E-Mail Address
If an e-mail address is entered, the middle digits of the credit card number will be sent to the e-mail address (the outside digits are stored in the database with the middle digits censored)

This sends part of the credit card number to the email address you specify, and stores the rest in the "Customer" database. You will have to log on to the Administrative module and match up the digits to manually process the order.

Payment Zone
If a zone is selected, only enable this payment method for that zone.
--none-- ▼

You can accept, say, checks or cash only in certain zones that you have established in the LOCATIONS/TAXES menu.

Set Order Status
Set the status of orders made with this payment module to this value
default ▼

Orders can be automatically set to "PENDING, PROCESSING or DELIVERED.

Sort order of display.
Sort order of display.
Lowest is displayed first.
0

You can enable multiple methods of payment; the sort order is a column on the PAYMENT MODULES screen. Zero will be displayed first, 1 next, etc.

Click the **Update button** when you are finished.

[update] [cancel]

Figure 68
The Payment Menu's
Credit Card Module

Cash On Delivery

Select Cash on Delivery if you are willing to send merchandise and have the postal service collect the funds for you.

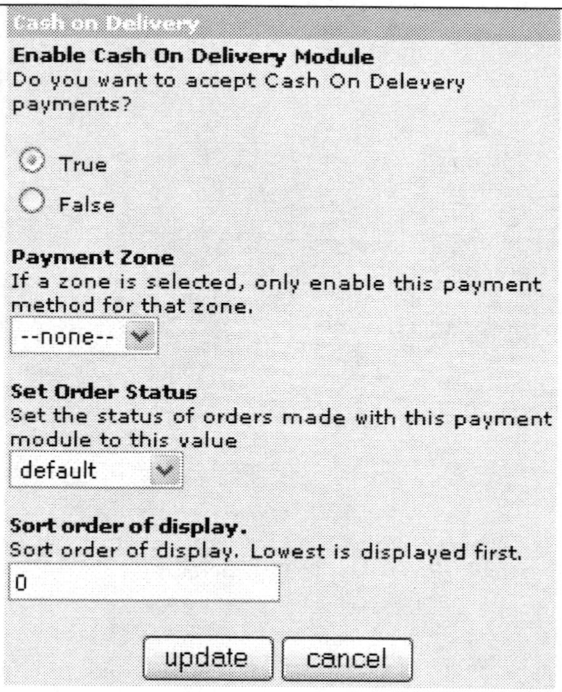

Enable Cash On Delivery Module
Do you want to accept Cash On Delevery payments?

○ True
○ False

You must select TRUE for this module to work.

Payment Zone
If a zone is selected, only enable this payment method for that zone.
--none--

You can accept, say, checks or cash only in certain zones that you have established in the LOCATIONS/TAXES menu.

Set Order Status
Set the status of orders made with this payment module to this value
default

Orders can be automatically set to "PENDING, PROCESSING or DELIVERED.

Sort order of display.
Sort order of display. Lowest is displayed first.
0

You can enable multiple methods of payment; the sort order is a column on the PAYMENT MODULES screen. Zero will be displayed first, 1 next, etc.

[update] [cancel]

Click the **Update button** when you are finished.

Figure 69
The Payment Menu's
Cash on Delivery Module

iPayment

iPayment is a payment service that allows the use of Euros and/or US Dollars. They accept VISA/MASTERCARD, AMERICAN EXPRESS, DISCOVER, DINERS CLUB, JCB and CARTE BLANCHE. Fees vary. Visit them at http://www.ipaymentinc.com/.

iPayment	
Enable iPayment Module Do you want to accept iPayment payments? ⦿ True ○ False	You must select TRUE for this module to work.
Account Number The account number used for the iPayment service `99999`	Enter the account number provided by iPayment.
User ID The user ID for the iPayment service `99999`	Enter the user ID provided by iPayment.
User Password The user password for the iPayment service `0`	Enter the user password provided by iPayment.
Transaction Currency The currency to use for credit card transactions ○ Always EUR ○ Always USD ⦿ Either EUR or USD, else EUR ○ Either EUR or USD, else USD	Enter the currency you wish to use to process your transactions.

Figure 70-a
The Payment Menu's
iPayment Module

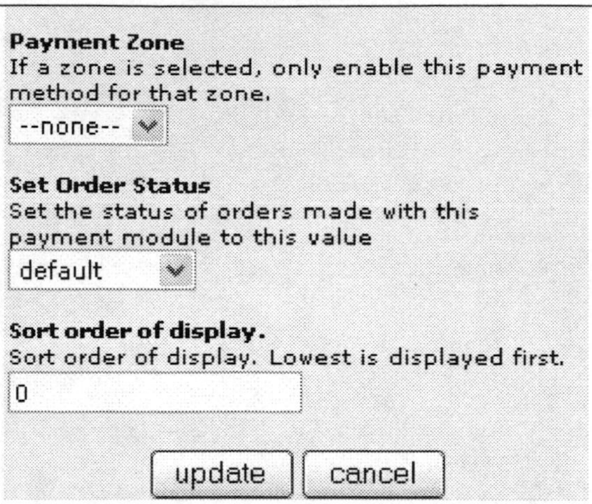

Payment Zone
If a zone is selected, only enable this payment method for that zone.

--none-- ▾

Set Order Status
Set the status of orders made with this payment module to this value

default ▾

Sort order of display.
Sort order of display. Lowest is displayed first.

0

[update] [cancel]

You can accept, say, checks or cash only in certain zones that you have established in the LOCATIONS/TAXES menu.

Orders can be automatically set to "PENDING, PROCESSING or DELIVERED.

You can enable multiple methods of payment; the sort order is a column on the PAYMENT MODULES screen. Zero will be displayed first, 1 next, etc.

Click the **Update button** when you are finished.

Figure 70-b
The Payment Menu's
iPayment Module

Check/Money Orders

If you are willing to accept personal checks or money orders by regular mail, enable this payment module. Your customers who place orders will automatically receive an email with your company name and address to mail a check, with a statement telling them the order will not be shipped until their check is received. Their order status should be set to pending.

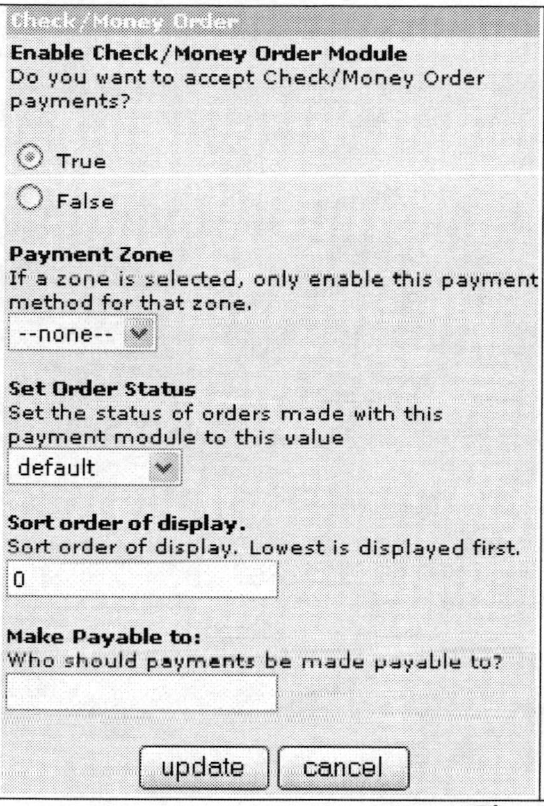

Check/Money Order

Enable Check/Money Order Module
Do you want to accept Check/Money Order payments?

◉ True

○ False

You must select TRUE for this module to work.

Payment Zone
If a zone is selected, only enable this payment method for that zone.

--none-- ▾

You can accept checks or money orders only in certain zones that you have established in the LOCATIONS/TAXES menu, for example, only in your city or state.

Set Order Status
Set the status of orders made with this payment module to this value

default ▾

Orders can be automatically set to "PENDING, PROCESSING or DELIVERED.

Sort order of display.
Sort order of display. Lowest is displayed first.

0

You can enable multiple methods of payment; the sort order is a column on the PAYMENT MODULES screen. Zero will be displayed first, 1 next, etc.

Make Payable to:
Who should payments be made payable to?

Specify to whom payments should be made, usually your company name or your name.

update   cancel

Click the **Update button** when you are finished.

Figure 71
The Payment Menu's
Check/Money Orders Module

Nochex

Nochex is the UK's number 1 email money service. With no setup fees, they charge 2.6% plus 20p for each transaction. Withdrawals over £50 are free; under £50 are 25p. Visit them at http://www.nochex.com.

Enable NOCHEX Module Do you want to accept NOCHEX payments? ⊙ True ○ False	You must select TRUE for this module to work.
E-Mail Address The e-mail address to use for the NOCHEX service `you@yourbusiness.com`	Enter the email address you used to sign up for the NOCHEX service.
Payment Zone If a zone is selected, only enable this payment method for that zone. `--none-- ▼`	You can accept checks or money orders only in certain zones that you have established in the LOCATIONS/TAXES menu, for example, only in your city or state.
Set Order Status Set the status of orders made with this payment module to this value `default ▼`	Orders can be automatically set to "PENDING, PROCESSING or DELIVERED.
Sort order of display. Sort order of display. Lowest is displayed first. `0`	You can enable multiple methods of payment; the sort order is a column on the PAYMENT MODULES screen. Zero will be displayed first, 1 next, etc.
`update` `cancel`	Click the **Update button** when you are finished.

Figure 72
The Payment Menu's
Nochex Module

PayPal

PayPal is the US's number 1 email money service. No setup fees, 2.9% + 30 cents for each transaction. Customers were formerly required to register, but no more. Visit them at http://www.paypal.com.

PayPal supports sending and receiving payments in five currencies: U.S. Dollars, Canadian Dollars, Euros, Pounds Sterling, or Yen.

In addition to the U.S., PayPal is available in the following countries (for updated listing see http://www.paypal.com/cgi-bin/webscr?cmd=_display-approved-signup-countries-outside):

In addition to the U.S., PayPal is now available in the following countries:

- Anguilla†
- Argentina
- Australia‡
- Austria*
- Belgium*
- Brazil
- Canada‡
- Chile
- China
- Costa Rica
- Denmark*
- Dominican Republic
- Ecuador
- Finland*
- France*
- Germany*
- Greece
- Hong Kong‡
- Iceland
- India
- Ireland*
- Israel
- Italy*
- Jamaica
- Japan‡
- Luxembourg
- Malaysia
- Mexico‡
- Monaco
- Netherlands*
- New Zealand*
- Norway*
- Portugal
- Singapore*
- South Korea*
- Spain‡
- Sweden‡
- Switzerland*
- Taiwan‡
- Thailand
- Turkey
- United Kingdom*
- Uruguay
- Venezuela

† Users in these countries are limited to sending money with their PayPal accounts. They may not receive payments.

‡ PayPal accepts withdrawals to local bank accounts in these countries. Users in any country may withdraw funds to a U.S. bank account.

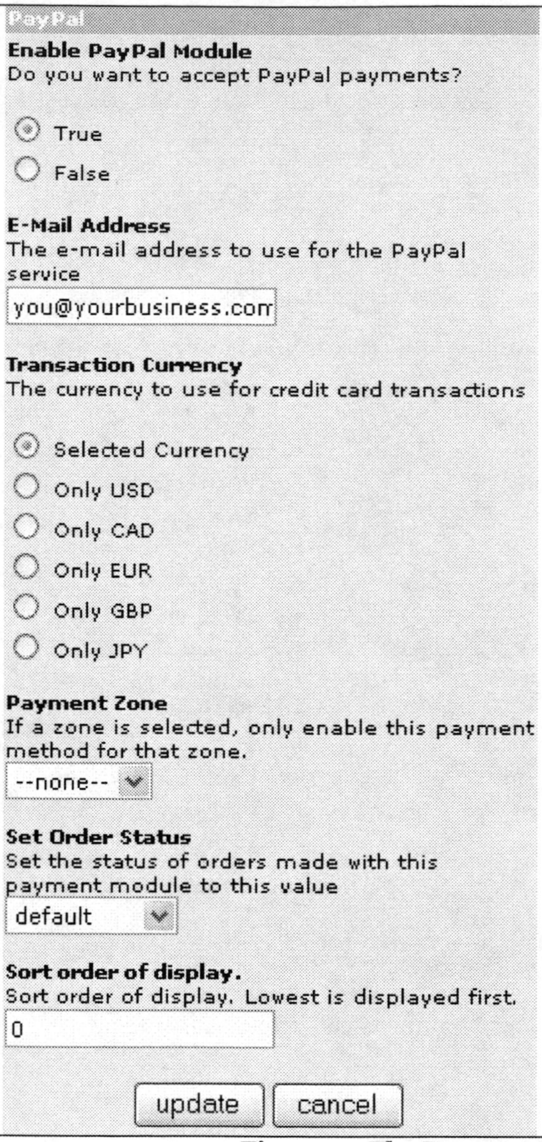

PayPal

Enable PayPal Module
Do you want to accept PayPal payments?

○ True
○ False

You must select TRUE for this module to work.

E-Mail Address
The e-mail address to use for the PayPal service

`you@yourbusiness.com`

Enter the email address you used to sign up for PayPal.

Transaction Currency
The currency to use for credit card transactions

○ Selected Currency
○ Only USD
○ Only CAD
○ Only EUR
○ Only GBP
○ Only JPY

Specify the currency or currencies you wish to use.

Payment Zone
If a zone is selected, only enable this payment method for that zone.

`--none--` ▾

You can accept checks or money orders only in certain zones that you have established in the LOCATIONS/TAXES menu, for example, only in your city or state.

Set Order Status
Set the status of orders made with this payment module to this value

`default` ▾

Orders can be automatically set to "PENDING, PROCESSING or DELIVERED.

Sort order of display.
Sort order of display. Lowest is displayed first.

`0`

You can enable multiple methods of payment; the sort order is a column on the PAYMENT MODULES screen. Zero will be displayed first, 1 next, etc.

[update] [cancel]

Click **Update** when you are finished.

Figure 73 The Payment Menu's PayPal Module

Optional Additional Setup for PayPal

PayPal users occasionally forget to finish their transaction by clicking the "Click Here to Continue" link, or by simply stopping and their transaction "times out" to prevent unauthorized users from using their computer. When this happens, the data are not returned to your osCommerce store, and you do not know what the customer purchased. In my own experience, about 15% of PayPal users have this problem.

You can prevent this problem with a few simple steps:

1. Log into PayPal.com and click Merchant Tools
2. Click Auto Return and select ON.
3. Enter the url http://www.yourwebsitename.com/catalog/checkout_success.php (enter the correct URL for your store)

You or your installer then need to edit one file. PayPal requires you to add some language to the screen the client returns to, such as:

"Thank you for your payment. Your transaction has been completed, and a receipt for your purchase has been emailed to you."

Open file catalog/includes/languages/english/checkout_success.php and

Search for	define('TEXT_SUCCESS', 'Your order has been successfully processed! Your products will arrive at their destination within 2-5 working days.');
and change it to	define('TEXT_SUCCESS', 'Thank you for your payment. Your transaction has been completed, and a receipt for your purchase has been emailed to you.');

You may of course edit the text to suit your needs, just be sure to not touch the ' ' that surrounds the text.

If you use an installer, be sure to ask them to add this language for you rather than getting into the PHP yourself.

2CheckOut

CheckOut is a fee-based payment processor with over 10,000 stores using its payment processing in its online shopping mall. $49 setup fee, $ 0.45 per Sale and 5.5% of Sale Amount. Services all countries except North Korea, Cuba, Libya, Iraq, Iran, Sudan and UNITA-Controlled Portions of Angola. Check them out at http://www.2checkout.com/.

One of the easiest and quickest account setups I have ever seen. I clicked to their site, filled out the form, and after a simple registration process received an email with my codes. *Within 15 minutes I had received my first order processed through this company!* Has a high transaction fee, but low initial setup and NO monthly or hidden fees. A breeze to set up. Highly recommended.

2CheckOut	
Enable 2CheckOut Module Do you want to accept 2CheckOut payments ⊙ True ○ False	You must select TRUE for this module to work.
Login/Store Number Login/Store Number used for the 2CheckOu service `1815/`	Enter the login or store number that was issued to you by 2CheckOut.
Transaction Mode Transaction mode used for the 2Checkout service ⊙ Test ○ Production	While you are testing, select TEST. This ensures the credit card numbers you enter will not be charged. YOU MUST CHANGE THIS TO PRODUCTION WHEN YOUR STORE IS LAUNCHED.
Merchant Notifications Should 2CheckOut e-mail a receipt to the s owner? ⊙ True ○ False	If you wish 2CheckOut to email a receipt to the customer, select TRUE. If you will manually email receipts, select FALSE.

Figure 74-a
The Payment Menu's
2CheckOut Module

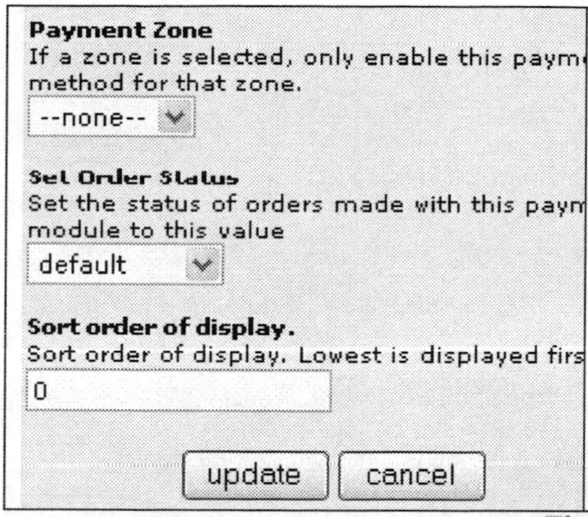

Payment Zone
If a zone is selected, only enable this payment method for that zone.

--none--

You can accept payments only in certain zones that you have established in the LOCATIONS/TAXES menu, for example, only in your city or state.

Set Order Status
Set the status of orders made with this payment module to this value

default

Orders can be automatically set to "PENDING, PROCESSING or DELIVERED."

Sort order of display.
Sort order of display. Lowest is displayed first

0

You can enable multiple methods of payment; the sort order is a column on the PAYMENT MODULES screen. Zero will be displayed first, 1 next, etc.

update   cancel

Click **Update** when you are finished.

Figure 74-b
The Payment Menu's
2CheckOut Module cont'd.

PsiGate

http://www.psigate.com – **PsiGate** is a popular Canadian payment processor. PSIGate provides Canadian merchants with Visa and MasterCard merchant IDs. They do not require initial deposits and their discount rate is very competitive. They do require a reserve fund of up to 5%. This allows Internet Businesses to receive a Merchant ID with very little upfront investment. All that PSiGate requires is a check of your credit history and trade references.

Enable PSiGate Module
Do you want to accept PSiGate payments?

- ◉ True
- ○ False

You must select TRUE for this module to work.

Merchant ID
Merchant ID used for the PSiGate service

teststorewithcard

Enter the merchant ID number that was issued to you by PsiGate.

Transaction Mode
Transaction mode to use for the PSiGate service

- ○ Production
- ◉ Always Good
- ○ Always Duplicate
- ○ Always Decline

While you are testing, select ALWAYS DECLINE. This ensures the credit card numbers you enter will not be charged. YOU MUST CHANGE THIS TO PRODUCTION WHEN YOUR STORE IS LAUNCHED.

Transaction Type
Transaction type to use for the PSiGate service

- ○ Sale
- ◉ PreAuth
- ○ PostAuth

Select the type of transaction you wish to use.

Credit Card Collection
Should the credit card details be collected locally or remotely at PSiGate?

- ◉ Local
- ○ Remote

If you have a secure server, you can select local, otherwise select remote.

Transaction Currency
The currency to use for credit card transactions

- ○ CAD
- ◉ USD

Specify Canadian or US Dollars.

PSiGate Payment Zone
If a zone is selected, only enable this payment method for that zone.

--none--

PSiGate Set Order Status
Set the status of orders made with this payment module to this value

default

PSiGate Sort order of display.
Sort order of display. Lowest is displayed first.

0

update   cancel

You can accept payments only in certain zones that you have established in the LOCATIONS/ TAXES menu, for example, only in your city or state.

Orders can be automatically set to "PENDING, PROCESSING or DELIVERED.

You can enable multiple methods of payment; the sort order is a column on the PAYMENT MODULES screen. Zero will be displayed first, 1 next, etc.

Click the **Update button** when you are finished.

SECPay

Another United Kingdom credit card and debit card processor. All accounts are subject to a one-time set up and connection fee of £50+ vat payable on registration. If your average product price is over £20 you may choose a fixed rate transaction fee of either £20 pounds and 39p per transaction (over 53 transactions per month) or £10 plus 20p per transaction (under 53 transaction per month).

If your average product price is over £20 and monthly sales under £1,111 you pay a percentage based transaction fee of £10 and 1.9%, if your monthly sales are over £1,111 you pay £20 and 1.0%.

http://www.secpay.com

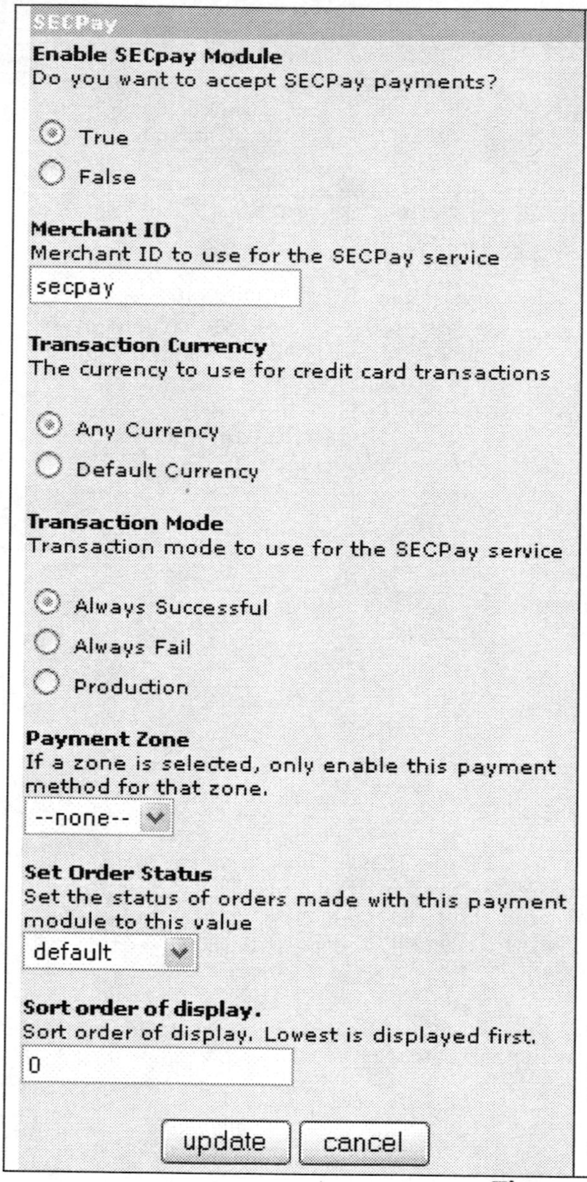

SECPay

Enable SECpay Module
Do you want to accept SECPay payments?

- ⦿ True
- ○ False

You must select TRUE for this module to work.

Merchant ID
Merchant ID to use for the SECPay service

`secpay`

Enter the merchant ID number that was issued to you by SECPay.

Transaction Currency
The currency to use for credit card transactions

- ⦿ Any Currency
- ○ Default Currency

Select the transaction currency you wish to use.

Transaction Mode
Transaction mode to use for the SECPay service

- ⦿ Always Successful
- ○ Always Fail
- ○ Production

While you are testing, select ALWAYS FAIL. This ensures the credit card numbers you enter will not be charged. YOU MUST CHANGE THIS TO PRODUCTION WHEN YOUR STORE IS LAUNCHED.

Payment Zone
If a zone is selected, only enable this payment method for that zone.

`--none--` ▾

You can accept payments only in certain zones that you have established in the LOCATIONS/TAXES menu, for example, only in your city or state.

Set Order Status
Set the status of orders made with this payment module to this value

`default` ▾

Orders can be automatically set to "PENDING, PROCESSING or DELIVERED.

Sort order of display.
Sort order of display. Lowest is displayed first.

`0`

You can enable multiple methods of payment; the sort order is a column on the PAYMENT MODULES screen. Zero will be displayed first, 1 next, etc.

[update] [cancel]

Click the **Update button** when you are finished.

Figure 76
The Payment Menu's
SECPay Module

Order Total

This menu allows you to customize what happens in the checkout process and rank (sort) the order in which checkout screens appear. Run through some test orders to see exactly how it works.

You will set the item you wish to display first as Item #1, the second item as #2, and so forth.

If you set two items with the same sort order, only one of them will display.

TIP: Give your customers enough information to complete the sale, but not so many screens that you overwhelm them with so much information that they get tired of going through the checkout process. Think of each screen as an obstacle in a physical store preventing the customer from buying.

To begin entering order total information, from the main **Administration menu**, click **Modules**.

Figure 77
Main Administration Menu
Modules Section

This brings you to the Modules menu in the left-hand column. Select **Order Total** from the **left-hand menu**.

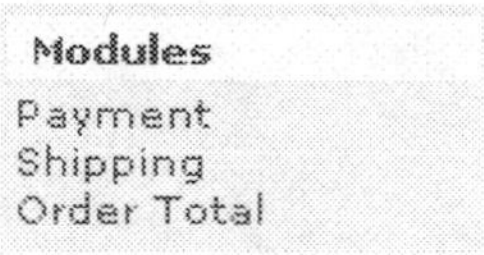

Modules
Payment
Shipping
Order Total

Figure 78
Left-hand column
Modules Menu

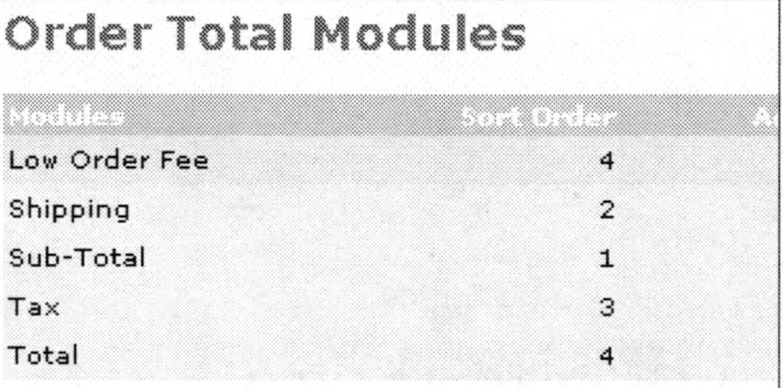

Order Total Modules

Modules	Sort Order	A
Low Order Fee	4	
Shipping	2	
Sub-Total	1	
Tax	3	
Total	4	

Allows a surcharge if an order is below a dollar amount you specify,

Display or hide shipping cost, specify free shipping and parameters.

Display or hide sub-total, tax, and/or total.

Figure 79
Modules Menu
Order Total Module

Low Order Fee

To implement a surcharge if an order is below a dollar amount you specify, from the Order Total Modules menu, select the **"i"** in the **Action** column, and the click the **EDIT button**.

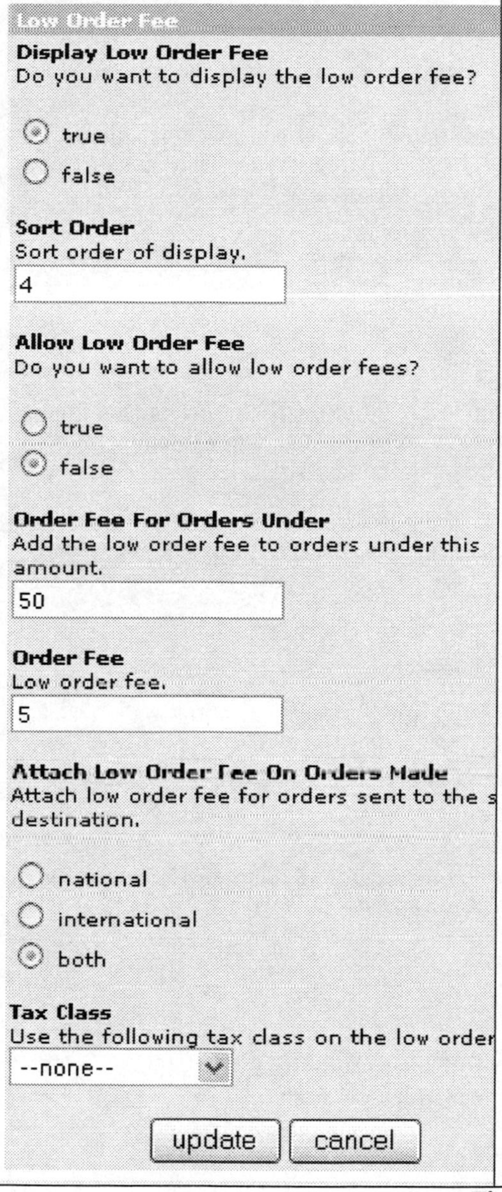

Low Order Fee

Display Low Order Fee
Do you want to display the low order fee?

◉ true

○ false

Must be set to true if you wish to display the low order fee. NOTE you must ALSO set "allow low order fee" to true for it to display.

Sort Order
Sort order of display.

4

Set the order in which the fee will display during the order checkout process.

Allow Low Order Fee
Do you want to allow low order fees?

○ true

◉ false

Must be set to true if you wish to implement low order fees.

Order Fee For Orders Under
Add the low order fee to orders under this amount.

50

Set a minimum order amount, under which the fee will be charged.

Order Fee
Low order fee.

5

Specify the amount of the low order fee surcharge.

Attach Low Order Fee On Orders Made
Attach low order fee for orders sent to the s destination.

○ national

○ international

◉ both

Specify whether the low order fee is to be charged to national orders only, international orders only, or both.

Tax Class
Use the following tax class on the low order

--none-- ⌄

Specify whether or not to charge tax on the low order fee.

[update] [cancel]

Click the **Update button** when you are finished.

Figure 80
Modules Menu
Low Order Fee Module

Shipping

To implement a shipping surcharge if an order is below a dollar amount you specify, to display or hide the shipping surcharge, or specify requirements for free shipping on some or all items, from the Order Total Modules menu, select the **"i"** in the **Action** column, and the click the **EDIT button**.

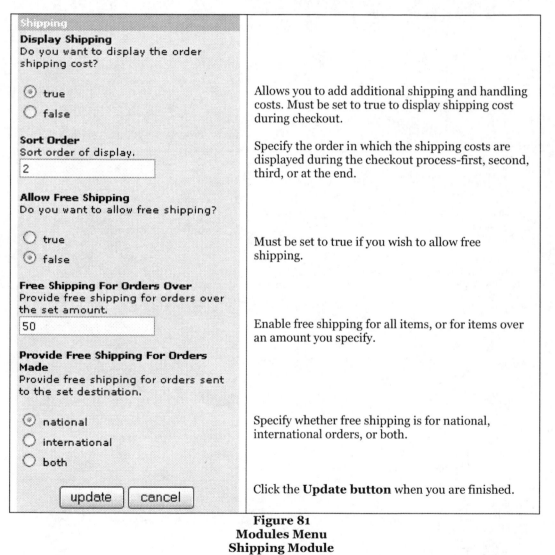

Allows you to add additional shipping and handling costs. Must be set to true to display shipping cost during checkout.

Specify the order in which the shipping costs are displayed during the checkout process-first, second, third, or at the end.

Must be set to true if you wish to allow free shipping.

Enable free shipping for all items, or for items over an amount you specify.

Specify whether free shipping is for national, international orders, or both.

Click the **Update button** when you are finished.

Figure 81
Modules Menu
Shipping Module

Sub-Total

To display or hide the order sub-total during the checkout process, from the Order Total Modules menu, select the **"i"** in the **Action** column, and the click the **EDIT button**.

 Subtotal can be a confusing and unnecessary screen during checkout. Set its sort order to zero unless it is absolutely necessary.

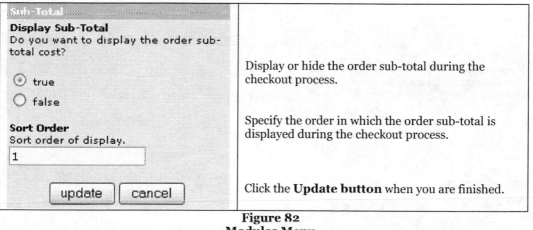

Figure 82
Modules Menu
Sub-Total Module

Tax

To display or hide the order tax during the checkout process, from the Order Total Modules menu, select the **"i"** in the **Action** column, and the click the **EDIT button**.

 Tax can be a confusing and unnecessary screen during check-out. Set its sort order to zero unless you believe it is absolutely necessary.

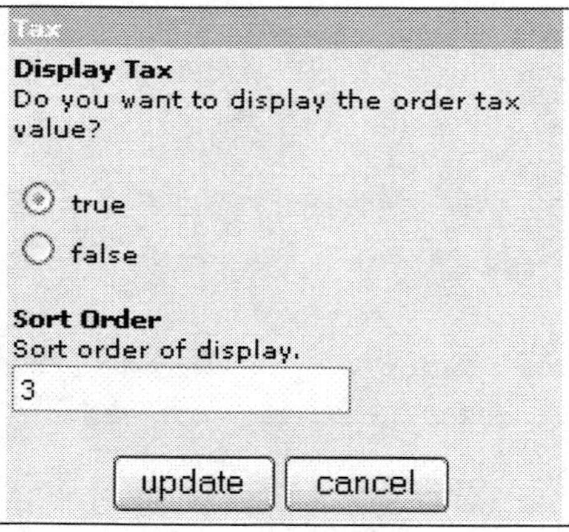

Tax	
Display Tax Do you want to display the order tax value? ⊙ true ○ false	Display or hide the tax amount during the check-out process.
Sort Order Sort order of display. 3	Specify the order in which the order sub-total is displayed during the checkout process.
update cancel	Click the **Update button** when you are finished.

Figure 83
Modules Menu
Tax Module

Total

To display or hide the order total during the checkout process, from the Order Total Modules menu, select the **"i"** in the **Action** column, and the click the **EDIT button**.

Total	
Display Total Do you want to display the total order value?	
⊙ true	Display or hide the order total during the checkout process.
○ false	
Sort Order Sort order of display.	Specify the order in which the order sub-total is displayed during the checkout process.
4	
[update] [cancel]	Click the **Update button** when you are finished.

Figure 84
Modules Menu
Total Module

Chapter

15

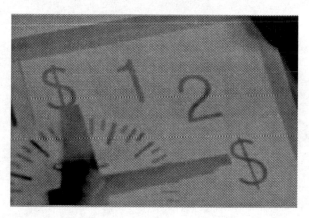

Shipping

In this chapter:

osCommerce can calculate your shipping costs using the method you prefer, and can automatically link to many shippers including Fedex, USPS, and UPS.

Level of difficulty: easy to medium.

Selecting the Shipping Method Right for You

Selecting a shipping method is a business decision you need to make. You will be able to fine-tune your decision as you go, and make changes "on-the-fly" so don't belabor your choice now. Remember you want on average to recoup the cost of your shipping, boxes, labels, and packaging. Occasionally you will go over or under. If it happens more than occasionally examine your costs and consider changing shipping methods, but otherwise don't worry about it.

Use the following chart to compare the different methods available. Find the columns that describe your merchandise most closely, and select the method that is appropriate for you:

		Heavy Items	Light Items	Large Items	Small Items	Variety	Similar	Inter-national	Ease of Install
Flat Rate	Single charge per order.		X		X		X		X
Per Item	Single charge per item	X		X		X		X	X
Table Rates	Shipping Charge increases with weight or price.	X	X	X		X			X
UPS	Has shipping zones across the US; charges increase with package weight, distance and speed of delivery.	X		X		X		X	
USPS	Single rate for delivery depending on package weight, distance and speed of delivery.		X		X	X	X	X	
Zones*	Distance-based. You establish as many zones as you wish and specify charges to each.	X	X	X	X	X	X	X	

*Requires additional editing by your installer or advanced developers to define the correct number of zones you need.

Once you have selected the method that is right for you, open up an account with that shipper if necessary before continuing.

Set Up Shipping

To set up shipping, from the main **Administration menu,** under **Modules,** click **Shipping.**

Figure 85
Main Administration Menu
Modules – Shipping Section

This brings you to Shipping. Here you find a list of shipping companies that can be automatically installed:

Shipping Modules

TIP: Click each of the modules and select EDIT to see how they are set up. Select the shipper and shipping modules that best fit your needs.

TIP: Shipping modules can easily conflict with one another, especially if you install multiple methods. INSTALL ONLY ONE AT A TIME, AND BE SURE TO TEST THOROUGHLY BEFORE INSTALLING ANOTHER.

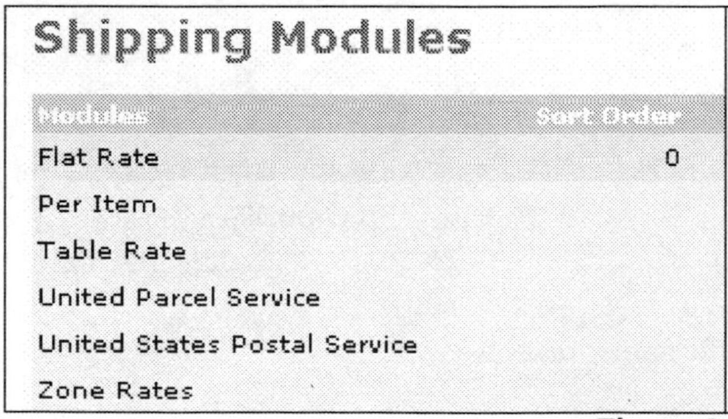

Shipping Modules		
Modules	**Sort Order**	
Flat Rate	0	Charge a flat fee.
Per Item		Charge per item.
Table Rate		Charge according to weight or price.
United Parcel Service		Connect to your UPS or USPS account.
United States Postal Service		Set different rates depending on different areas or zones, such as city, state, county or country.
Zone Rates		

Figure 86
Modules Menu
Shipping Modules Section

Flat Rate Shipping

Select Flat Rate Shipping if you wish to charge a single per-order shipping fee to all customers, regardless of what product(s) they ordered or how many.

Flat Rate **Enable Flat Shipping** Do you want to offer flat rate shipping? ⊙ True ○ False	TRUE must be selected if you wish to enable flat rate shipping.
Shipping Cost The shipping cost for all orders using this shipping method. [5.00]	How much is the flat rate you wish to charge.
Tax Class Use the following tax class on the shipping fee. [--none-- ▾]	If you are required to charge tax on shipping as well as your goods, select it here.
Shipping Zone If a zone is selected, only enable this shipping method for that zone. [--none-- ▾]	If you are required to charge tax on shipping to a selected zone, such as within your city or state, select it here.
Sort Order Sort order of display. [0] [update] [cancel]	If you will offer more than one shipping method, select the order in which it will be displayed. Click the **Update button** when you are finished.

Figure 87
Modules Menu
Flat Rate Shipping Module

Per Item Shipping

Select Per Item Shipping if you wish to charge a separate shipping fee for each item. For example, shipping for one book is $5, 2 books is $10, and so on. Be careful if you choose this method and ship internationally.

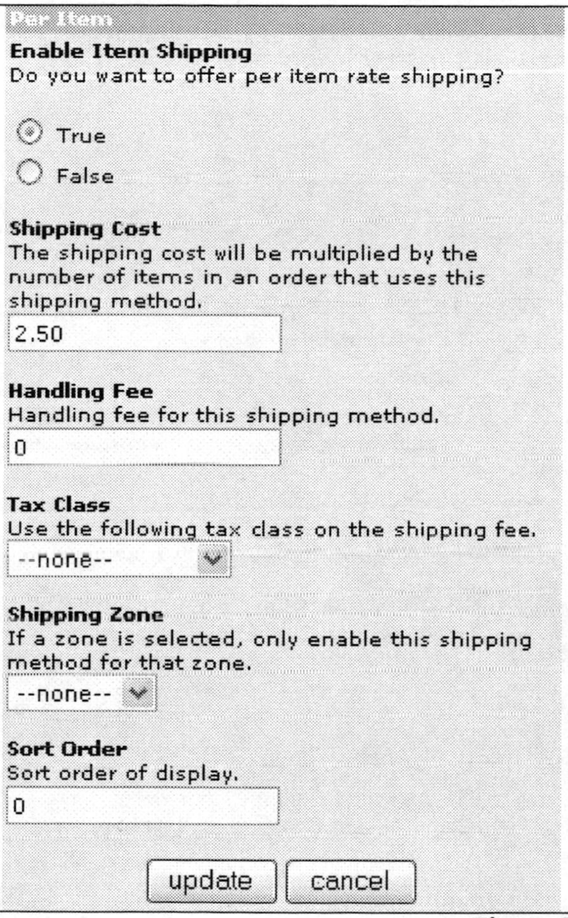

Per Item

Enable Item Shipping
Do you want to offer per item rate shipping?

○ True

○ False

TRUE must be selected if you wish to charge shipping cost on a per item basis.

Shipping Cost
The shipping cost will be multiplied by the number of items in an order that uses this shipping method.

2.50

How much is the shipping cost for each item.

Handling Fee
Handling fee for this shipping method.

0

If you wish to include a per-order handling fee as well, include it here.

Tax Class
Use the following tax class on the shipping fee.

--none--

If are required to charge tax on shipping as well as your goods, select it here.

Shipping Zone
If a zone is selected, only enable this shipping method for that zone.

--none--

If you are required to charge tax on shipping to a selected zone, such as within your city or state, select it here.

Sort Order
Sort order of display.

0

If you will offer more than one shipping method, select the order in which it will be displayed.

update   cancel

Click the **Update button** when you are finished.

Figure 88
Modules Menu
Per Item Shipping Module

Table Rates Shipping

Select Table Rate Shipping if you wish to charge the shipping cost based on either the total cost or weight of your items. Click either weight or price, then specify the ranges in the Shipping Table. NOTE: This method also allows you to set a separate per-order handling fee in addition to the weight or cost.

Table Rate	
Enable Table Method Do you want to offer table rate shipping? ⦿ True ○ False	TRUE must be selected if you wish to enable table rate shipping.
Shipping Table The shipping cost is based on the total cost or weight of items. Example: 25:8.50,50:5.50,etc.. Up to 25 charge 8.50, from there to 50 charge 5.50, etc `25:8.50,50:5.50,10000`	How much is the table rate. Example: up to 25 pounds, charge 8.50 is expressed as 25:8.50.
Table Method The shipping cost is based on the order total or the total weight of the items ordered. ⦿ weight ○ price	Do you wish to charge shipping on the amount or weight of items ordered.
Handling Fee Handling fee for this shipping method. `0`	If you wish to include a per-order handling fee as well, include it here.

- Table continued on next page -

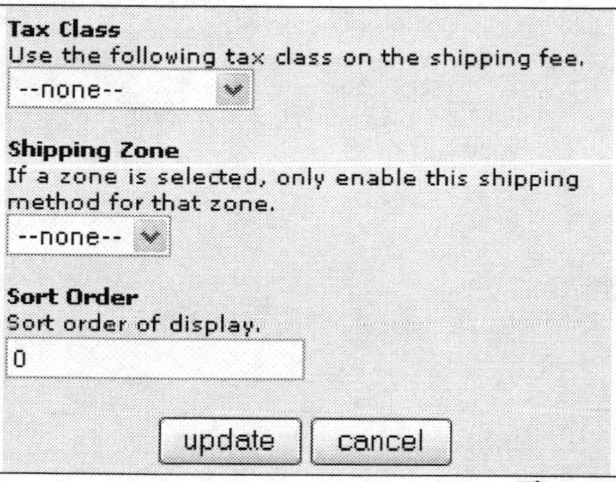

Tax Class
Use the following tax class on the shipping fee.

--none--

Shipping Zone
If a zone is selected, only enable this shipping method for that zone.

--none--

Sort Order
Sort order of display.

0

update   cancel

If you are required to charge tax on shipping as well as your goods, select it here.

If you are required to charge tax on shipping to a selected zone, such as within your city or state, select it here.

If you will offer more than one shipping method, select the order in which it will be displayed.

Click the **Update button** when you are finished.

Figure 89
Modules Menu
Table Rates Shipping Module

UPS Shipping

Select UPS Shipping if you have a UPS shipping account with daily pickup. UPS recommends speaking with your UPS rep to get the tools you need. For more information see
http://www.ec.ups.com/ecommerce/gettools/gtools_intro.html

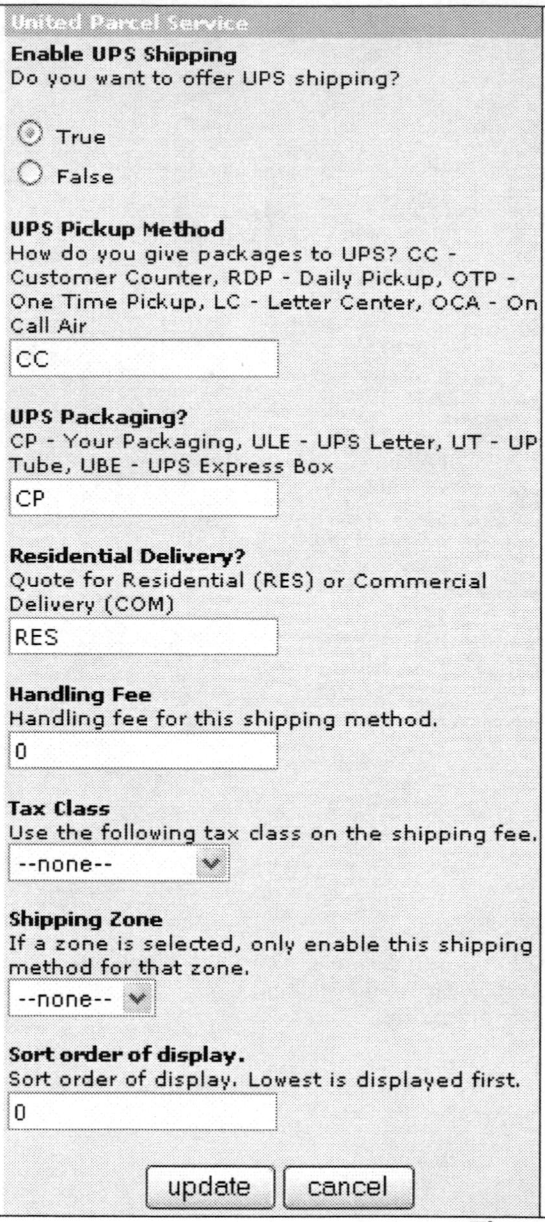

United Parcel Service

Enable UPS Shipping
Do you want to offer UPS shipping?

◉ True
○ False

TRUE must be selected if you wish to link to your UPS shipping account.

UPS Pickup Method
How do you give packages to UPS? CC - Customer Counter, RDP - Daily Pickup, OTP - One Time Pickup, LC - Letter Center, OCA - On Call Air

```
CC
```

Enter the code for the type of account pickup you have.

UPS Packaging?
CP - Your Packaging, ULE - UPS Letter, UT - UP Tube, UBE - UPS Express Box

```
CP
```

Enter the type of packaging you use.

Residential Delivery?
Quote for Residential (RES) or Commercial Delivery (COM)

```
RES
```

Do you deliver to residential or commercial?

Handling Fee
Handling fee for this shipping method.

```
0
```

If you wish to include a per-order handling fee as well, include it here.

Tax Class
Use the following tax class on the shipping fee.

--none-- ⌄

If you are required to charge tax on shipping as well as your goods, select it here.

Shipping Zone
If a zone is selected, only enable this shipping method for that zone.

--none-- ⌄

If you are required to charge tax on shipping to a selected zone, such as within your city or state, select it here.

Sort order of display.
Sort order of display. Lowest is displayed first.

```
0
```

If you will offer more than one shipping method, select the order in which it will be displayed.

[update] [cancel]

Click the **Update button** when you are finished.

Figure 90
Modules Menu
UPS Shipping Module

US Postal Service Shipping

Select US Postal Service Shipping if you have an account with the US Postal Service for shipping to customers. Register for your account on the web at http://www.usps.com/webtools/.

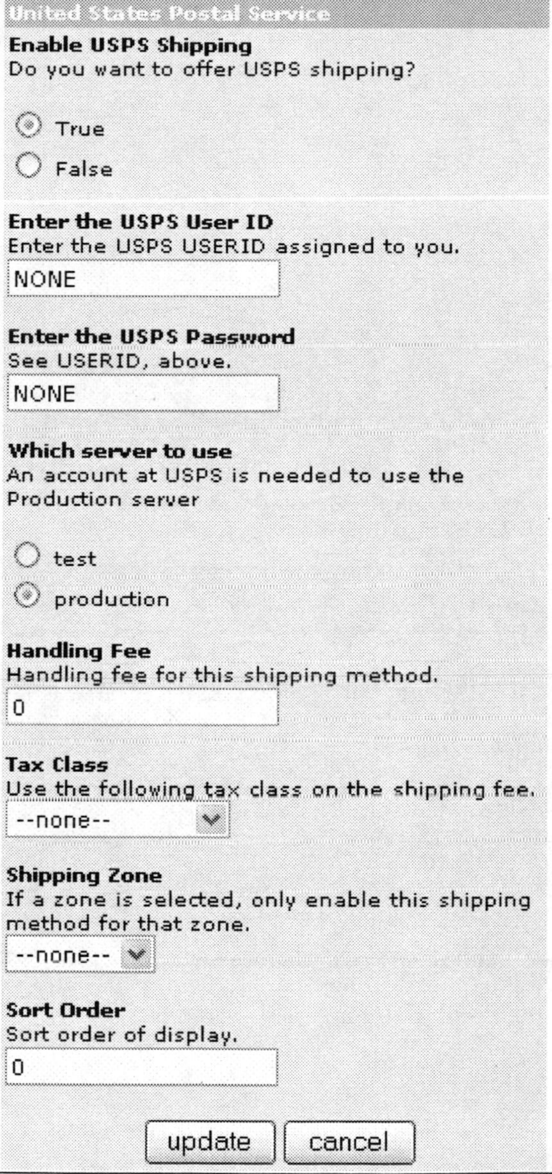

United States Postal Service

Enable USPS Shipping
Do you want to offer USPS shipping?

○ True
○ False

TRUE must be selected if you wish to link to your USPS shipping account.

Enter the USPS User ID
Enter the USPS USERID assigned to you.

NONE

Enter your USPS User ID.

Enter the USPS Password
See USERID, above.

NONE

Enter your USPS password.

Which server to use
An account at USPS is needed to use the Production server

○ test
○ production

While you are testing, select TEST. This ensures the account numbers you enter will not be charged. YOU MUST CHANGE THIS TO PRODUCTION WHEN YOUR STORE IS LAUNCHED.

Handling Fee
Handling fee for this shipping method.

0

f you wish to include a per-order handling fee as well, include it here.

Tax Class
Use the following tax class on the shipping fee.

--none--

If you are required to charge tax on shipping as well as your goods, select it here.

Shipping Zone
If a zone is selected, only enable this shipping method for that zone.

--none--

If you are required to charge tax on shipping to a selected zone, such as within your city or state, select it here.

Sort Order
Sort order of display.

0

If you will offer more than one shipping method, select the order in which it will be displayed.

update   cancel

Click the **Update button** when you are finished.

Figure 91 - Modules Menu
US Post Office Shipping Module

Zone Rates Shipping

Select Zone Rate Shipping if you wish to charge a different rate depending on the recipient's distance from you. For example, one rate inside your city, another in your state, another US, another International. This works extremely well if you use different shippers depending on the zone.

TIP: The default number of zones in the standard installation is only 1 Zone. DOH!

You must contact your installer and ask them to add the number of extra zones you desire BEFORE attempting to use zone rates.

Directions for adding the correct number of zones:

1. Open the Administrative Module and select Modules-Shipping.
2. Go to Zone Based Rates and make sure it is **NOT installed**. If it is, select REMOVE and exit from the Admin Module.
3. Open up the file catalog/includes/modules/shipping/zones.php and

Search for this line	$this->num_zones = 1;
Change only the text shown in **bold:**	$this->num_zones = 3;

Note that you should change the number of zones (num_zones) to however many zones you desire.

4. Return to the Administrative Module and continue setting up zones as shown below.

Zone Rates

Enable Zones Method
Do you want to offer zone rate shipping?

⦿ True

◯ False

TRUE must be selected if you wish to enable zone-based shipping.

Tax Class
Use the following tax class on the shipping fee.

--none--

If you are required to charge tax on shipping as well as your goods, select it here.

Sort Order
Sort order of display.

0

If you will offer more than one shipping method, select the order in which it will be displayed.

Zone 1 Countries
Comma separated list of two character ISO country codes that are part of Zone 1.

US,CA

Enter the list of countries to which you will ship in Zone 1.

Zone 1 Shipping Table
Shipping rates to Zone 1 destinations based on a group of maximum order weights. Example: 3:8.50,7:10.50,... Weights less than or equal to 3 would cost 8.50 for Zone 1 destinations.

3:8.50,7:10.50,99:20.0

Enter the weights and charges for Zone 1. Example: up to 3 pounds, zone 1 cost is 8.50 expressed as 3:8.50.

Zone 1 Handling Fee
Handling Fee for this shipping zone

0

If you will charge a per-order handling fee for this zone, enter it here.

Click the **Update button** when you are finished.

update   cancel

After you select update, return again to add Zone 2 and any additional zones.

Figure 92
Modules Menu
Zone Rate Shipping Module

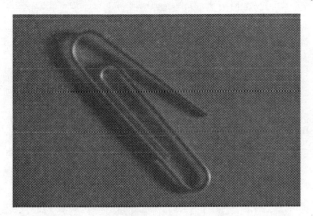

Website Housekeeping

In this chapter:

This is the stuff that is just not covered anywhere else. Use this chapter only when you need it.

Level of difficulty: easy to medium.

Reviews

Sometimes you'll get an odd review from a customer that you need to edit or remove. Maybe kids got on your site or a competitor who hates you – you need to read your own reviews to make sure this hasn't happened. This is where you fix it.

From the **Main Administrative screen**, go to **Catalog**, then from the left-hand **Catalog Menu** select **Reviews**. From there you may select the **EDIT button** or **DELETE button**.

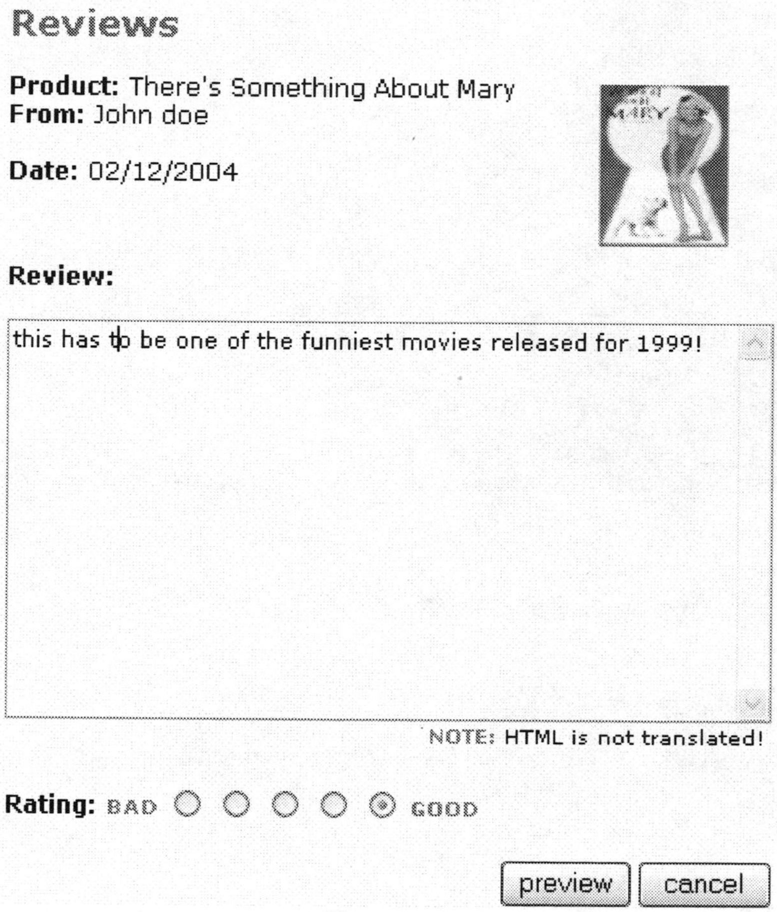

Reviews

Product: There's Something About Mary
From: John doe

Date: 02/12/2004

Review:

this has to be one of the funniest movies released for 1999!

NOTE: HTML is not translated!

Rating: BAD ○ ○ ○ ○ ⊙ GOOD

preview   cancel

Figure 93
Catalog Menu
Edit Reviews Module

Specials

If you want to offer certain products on sale, this is where you do it. You may leave it on permanent special, or have it automatically revert back to the regular price on a certain date.

From the **Main Administrative screen**, go to **Catalog**, then from the left-hand **Catalog Menu** select **Specials**. From there you may select buttons to add a **NEW PRODUCT**, **EDIT** or **DELETE**.

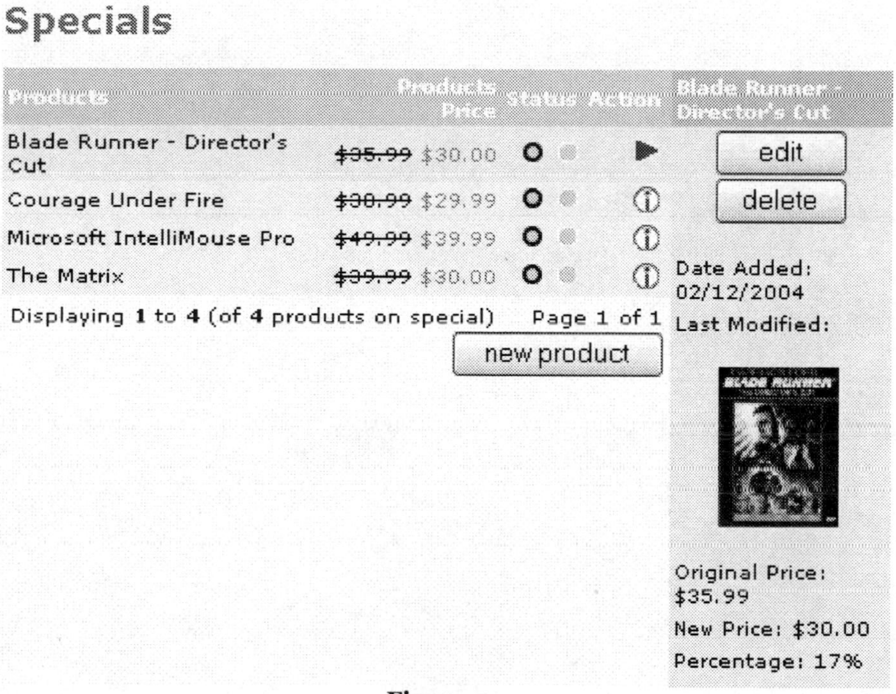

Figure 94
Catalog Menu
Specials Module

Create a New Special

Specials

Product: A Bug's Life ($35.99) ▼

Special Price: [   ]

Expiry Date: [   ][   ][   ] ▷

Specials Notes: insert   cancel

- You can enter a percentage to deduct in the Specials Price field, for example: **20%**
- If you enter a new price, the decimal separator must be a '.' (decimal-point), example: **49.99**
- Leave the expiry date empty for no expiration

Figure 95
Catalog Menu
Create New Special Module

Edit an existing Special

From the **Main Administrative screen**, go to **Catalog**, then from the left-hand Catalog Menu select **Specials**, then **EDIT**.

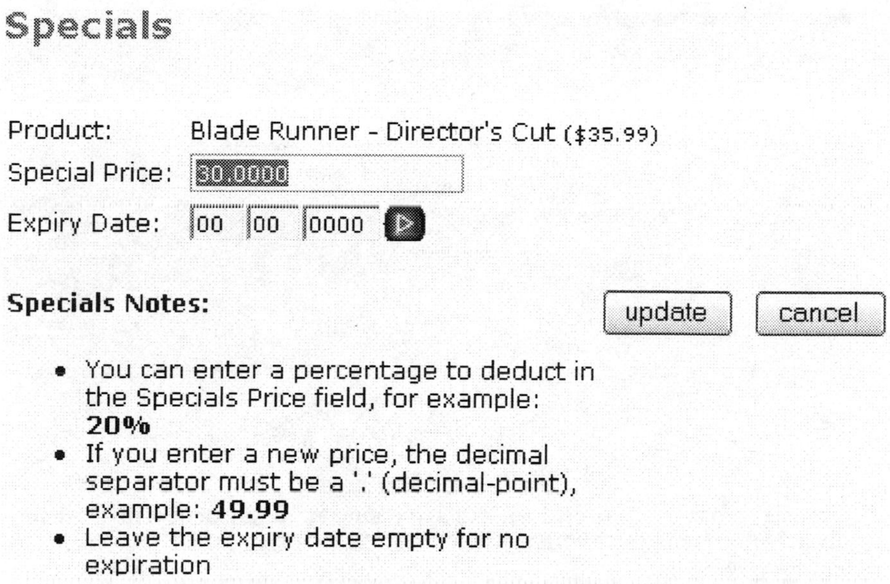

Specials

Product: Blade Runner - Director's Cut ($35.99)
Special Price: [30.0000]
Expiry Date: [00] [00] [0000] ▷

Specials Notes: [update]   [cancel]

- You can enter a percentage to deduct in the Specials Price field, for example: **20%**
- If you enter a new price, the decimal separator must be a '.' (decimal-point), example: **49.99**
- Leave the expiry date empty for no expiration

Figure 96
Catalog Menu
Edit Existing Special Section

Delete an Existing Special

From the **Main Administrative screen**, go to **Catalog**, then from the left-hand **Catalog Menu** select **Specials, then DELETE**.

Products Expected

If you have listed a date in the future in a product's description area, rather than having to go to each individual product to change the information when your stock comes in, you may manage them all from this screen in one simple process.

From the **Main Administrative screen**, go to **Catalog**, then from the left-hand **Catalog** Menu select **Products Expected.**

Highlight an individual product name to **edit** it.

Products Expected

Products	Date Expected	Action
Displaying **0** to **0** (of **0** products expected)		Page 0 of 0

Figure 97
Catalog Menu
Products Expected Module

Currencies

To change or add currencies, from the **Main Administrative screen**, find **Localization**, then click **Currencies**. From here you may add a **NEW CURRENCY, EDIT**, or **DELETE** a currency.

TIP: The default currency is the US Dollar. You do not need to add or edit for this to take effect.

Edit a Currency:

To edit a currency, from the **Main Administrative screen**, find **Localization**, then click **Currencies**, then the **EDIT button**.

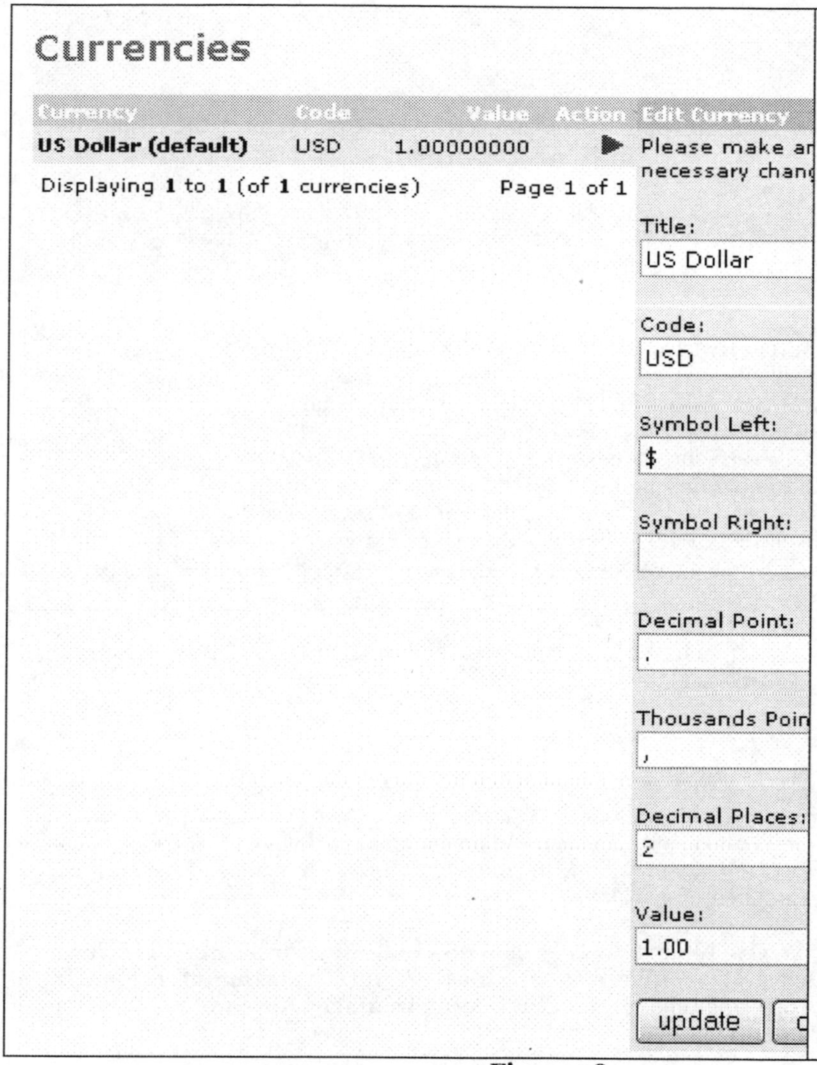

Currencies

Currency	Code	Value	Action	Edit Currency
US Dollar (default)	USD	1.00000000	▶	Please make an necessary chang

Displaying 1 to 1 (of 1 currencies)   Page 1 of 1

Title:

US Dollar

Specify the currency title

Code:

USD

What abbreviation (code) do you wish to use

Symbol Left:

$

Sign to be used and hether the symbol is placed on the left or right

Symbol Right:

Decimal Point:

.

The indicator for the decimal point

Thousands Poin

,

The indicator for thousands points

Decimal Places:

2

How many decimal places to use

Value:

1.00

Indicate the value.

Click the Update button when you are finished.

update   c

Figure 98
The Localization Menu's
Edit Currencies Module

Tools Menu

The Tools menu is like the Swiss Army Knife of osCommerce: some tools you will use frequently, others you will ponder their purpose and probably never need them.

From the **Main Administrative screen**, select **Tools**. This will bring you to the left-column **TOOLS** menu, as follows:

Tools	
Database Backup	Run your weekly backups here. IMPORTANT!
Banner Manager	Run banner ads, schedule them, specify run frequency, review stats.
Cache Control	Set or clear caches for various sections of the database.
Define Languages	Define languages for specific pages.
File Manager	EDIT FILES such as conditions, shipping info, privacy.
Send Email	Write and send emails to one/all customers or newsletter subscribers.
Newsletter Manage	Write, preview, lock/unlock, delete, send or save newsletters.
Server Info	Server name, path, operating system, and software versions.
Who's Online	See how many customers are using your store right now and where they are.

Figure 99
The Left-Hand Tools Menu

Database Backup

It is important that you regularly back up your database for good records management. This ideally means printing a copy of each order as it comes in, and a full digital backup of the database each week. If your database ever crashes, you will understand what I mean. Imagine that it happened, and take all precautions so you never need them.

TIP: It is wise to have weekly backups in both your admin/backups directory AND an identical copy on your personal computer. Printing a paper copy of each order as they come in makes for good records management.

TIP: Your database may also be automatically backed up by your ISP. Contact them in case of a disaster.

If you are your own ISP you will have to perform your own backups.

To set up or run backups you must first create the file directory and set file permissions where the backups are to be located. If you have not done this you will see an ERROR MESSAGE at the top of your screen.

The default directory where osCommerce will attempt to store backups is admin/backups/

TIP: If you do not know how to create new directories or set file permissions, ask your installer to do it for you so you can back up your website.

From the **Main Administrative screen**, select **Tools**. From the left-column **TOOLS** menu, select **Database Backup** and click the **BACKUP** button.

Select the type of backup you wish, **GZIP, ZIP** or pure **SQL**, and click the **DOWNLOAD ONLY** button if you wish to download to your computer's hard drive. A pop up box will ask you to select the folder to put it in.

Do not interrupt the process, it only takes a few minutes. Keep your hands off the keyboard as the backup is progressing to ensure the integrity of your data.

Banner Manager

If you wish to run advertisements for other companies on your website, this is the place to do it. The banner manager allows you to run banner ads in your footers, schedule them, specify how frequently they run, and review their usage statistics.

Your installer should set up banners for you; then adding or updating banners is easy. These instructions cover adding or updating ONLY.

From the **Main Administrative screen**, select **Tools**. From the left-column **TOOLS** menu, select **Banner Manager.**

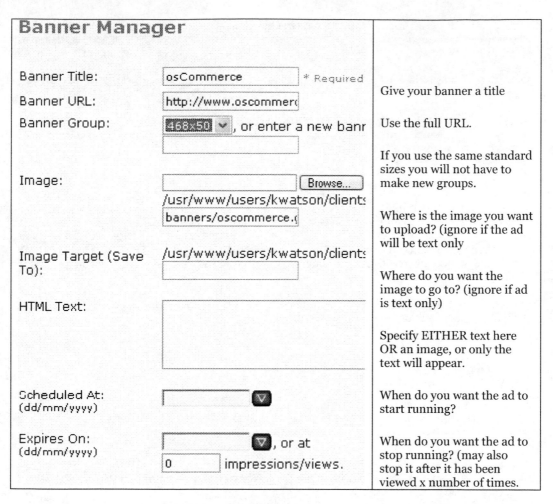

Figure 100
The Tools Menu's
Banner Manager Module

Cache Control

Cache control is for technical users only. We include it here in case your installer or technical consultant asks you to reset your cache.

A cache allows the website to appear to work faster by keeping a copy of frequently used, memory intensive items in the same place. The cache control allows you to clear your cache for the Categories, Manufacturers, and Also Purchased boxes. If you have problems with any of these items you may be asked to clear your cache.

From the **Main Administrative screen**, select **Tools**. From the left-column **TOOLS** menu, select **Cache Control**. To clear the cache, simply click the **"Recycle" symbol** in the **Action column** so the electrons will be recycled and not be wasted:

Cache Control

Cache Blocks	Date Created	Action
Categories Box	01/12/2004 15:12:02	♻
Manufacturers Box	01/12/2004 13:28:37	♻
Also Purchased Module	02/13/2004 16:44:48	♻
Cache Directory: /tmp/		

Figure 101
The Tools Menu's
Cache Control Module

Define Languages

If you use more than one language on your website, you can define in which language each page of your website will be displayed.

From the **Main Administrative screen**, select **Tools**. From the left-column **TOOLS** menu, select **Define Languages.** Open the drop-down language box to change the language.

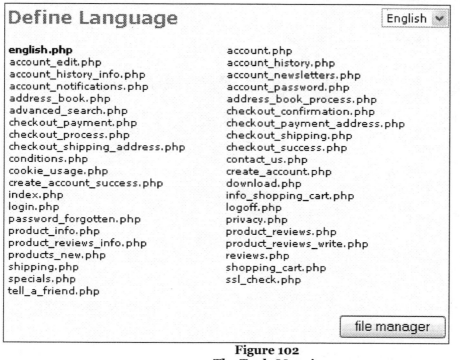

Figure 102
The Tools Menu's
Define Languages Module

File Manager

The File Manager allows you to EDIT FILES such as conditions, shipping info, privacy. If your installer has set appropriate permissions, you can also add files, create folders, delete, review file or folder permissions and more.

FILE MANAGER is also covered in the QUICK START and PRODUCTS MANAGEMENT chapters.

CAUTION: Follow directions exactly, this is easy to mess up!

BE SURE TO MAKE A BACKUP FIRST BEFORE EDITING ANY TEXT!

From the **Main Administrative screen**, select **Tools**. From the left-column **TOOLS** menu, select **File Manager.** Click the file folder or file name of the file you wish to edit.

File Manager

/usr/www/users/kwatson/clients/nanas-closet/

Name	Size	Permissions	User	Group	Last Modified	Action
📁 admin		drwxr-xr-x	kwatson	users	02/12/2004 15:47:21	
📁 download		drwxr-xr-x	kwatson	users	02/12/2004 15:47:27	
📁 images		drwxrwxrwx	kwatson	users	02/12/2004 17:31:58	
📁 includes		drwxr-xr-x	kwatson	users	02/12/2004 15:54:37	
📁 pub		drwxr-xr-x	kwatson	users	02/12/2004 15:56:16	
.htaccess	876 bytes	-rw-r--r--	kwatson	users	06/12/2003 12:53:20	
account.php	11,418 bytes	-rw-r--r--	kwatson	users	06/10/2003 01:03:52	
account_edit.php	12,039 bytes	-rw-r--r--	kwatson	users	06/10/2003 01:03:52	
account_history.php	7,530 bytes	-rw-r--r--	kwatson	users	06/10/2003 01:03:52	
account_history_info.php	11,563 bytes	-rw-r--r--	kwatson	users	06/10/2003 01:03:52	
account_newsletters.php	7,188 bytes	-rw-r--r--	kwatson	users	06/06/2003 01:23:52	
redirect.php	2,841 bytes	-rw-r--r--	kwatson	users	06/06/2003 01:31:32	
reviews.php	7,494 bytes	-rw-r--r--	kwatson	users	06/10/2003 01:03:56	
shipping.php	3,563 bytes	-rw-r--r--	kwatson	users	06/06/2003 01:26:24	
shopping_cart.php	11,507 bytes	-rw-r--r--	kwatson	users	06/10/2003 01:03:56	
specials.php	5,711 bytes	-rw-r--r--	kwatson	users	06/10/2003 00:35:34	
ssl_check.php	3,259 bytes	-rw-r--r--	kwatson	users	03/11/2003 01:32:20	
stylesheet.css	5,820 bytes	-rw-r--r--	kwatson	users	02/12/2004 17:45:24	
tell_a_friend.php	10,239 bytes	-rw-r--r--	kwatson	users	06/11/2003 19:35:02	

| reset | | upload | new file | new folder |

Figure 103
The Tools Menu's
File Manager Module

Send Email

Send email allows you to write and send emails to one/all customers or newsletter subscribers.

 TIP: If you wish to save a message as a form for future use, use the Newsletter Manager instead

From the **Main Administrative screen**, select **Tools**. From the left-column **TOOLS** menu, select **Send Email.** From the drop box, select the group name to whom you wish to mail, type the message, and click the **SEND button**:

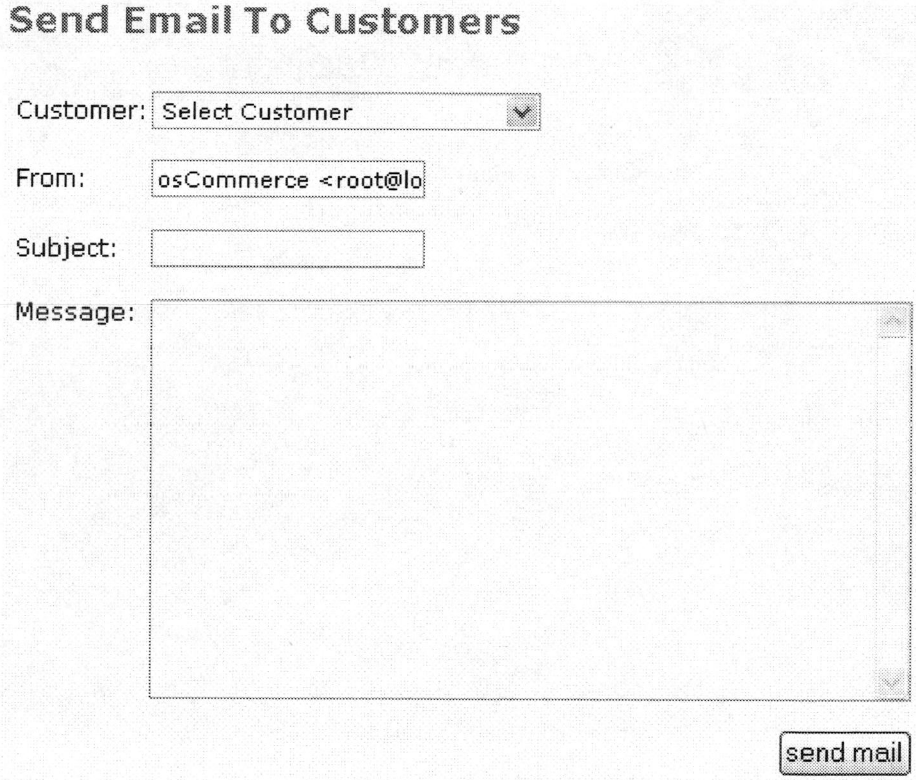

Send Email To Customers

Customer: Select Customer

From: osCommerce <root@lo

Subject:

Message:

send mail

Figure 104
The Tools Menu's
Send Email to Customers Module

Newsletter Manager

Newsletter Manager allows you to write, preview, lock/unlock to prevent accidental mailouts, delete, send or save newsletters. The newsletters in the standard version of osCommerce are TEXT ONLY.

From the **Main Administrative screen**, select **Tools**. From the left-column **TOOLS** menu, select **Newsletter Manager.** To compose a new newsletter, click the **NEW NEWSLETTER** button.

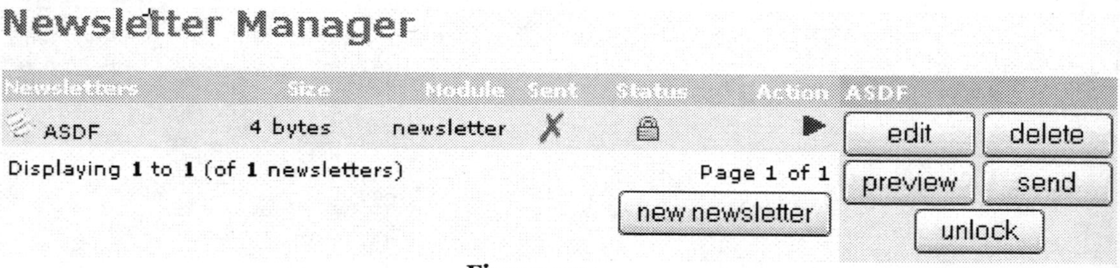

Newsletter Manager

Newsletters	Size	Module	Sent	Status	Action	ASDF	
ASDF	4 bytes	newsletter	✗	🔒	▶	edit	delete

Displaying **1** to **1** (of **1** newsletters)   Page 1 of 1

preview   send

new newsletter   unlock

Figure 105
The Tools Menu's
Newsletter Manager Module

Newsletter Manager

Module: newsletter ⌄

Newsletter Title: ASDF   * Required

Content:

update   cancel

Figure 106

**The Tools Menu's
Edit Newsletter Module**

After you click the **SAVE** button, it brings you back to the **Newsletter Manager** screen.

To send your newsletter, you must select the **LOCK** button. Once it is locked you may **EDIT, DELETE, PREVIEW, UNLOCk** or **SEND**.

TIP: It is always a good idea to PREVIEW your newsletter before sending.

Server Info

The Server Info menu tells you server name, path, operating system, and software versions. Your installer or technical consultant may ask you this information sometime during troubleshooting.

From the **Main Administrative screen**, select **Tools**. From the left-column **TOOLS** menu, select **Server Info.**

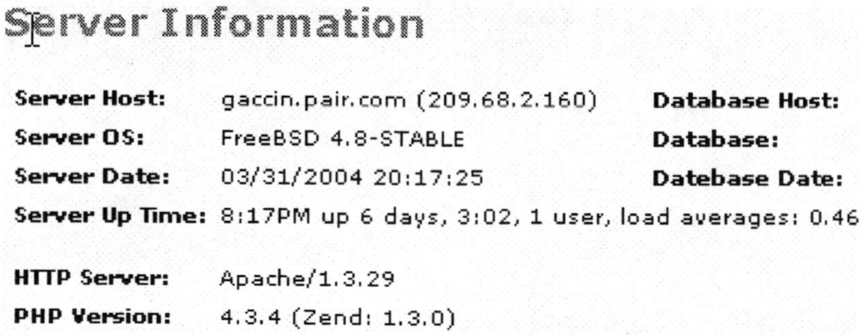

Server Information

Server Host:	gaccin.pair.com (209.68.2.160)	**Database Host:**
Server OS:	FreeBSD 4.8-STABLE	**Database:**
Server Date:	03/31/2004 20:17:25	**Datebase Date:**
Server Up Time:	8:17PM up 6 days, 3:02, 1 user, load averages: 0.46	

HTTP Server: Apache/1.3.29
PHP Version: 4.3.4 (Zend: 1.3.0)

**Figure 107
The Tools Menu's Server Information Module**

Who's Online

This fun module allows you to see how many customers are using your store right now, where they are, what they are clicking. Wow, look at all the people in the store! If you are going to perform maintenance, it is a good idea to check this to see if anybody is in the store before you temporarily take the site down.

From the **Main Administrative screen**, select **Tools**. From the left-column **TOOLS** menu, select **Who's Online.**

Who's Online

Online	ID	Full Name	IP Address	Entry Time	Last Click	Last URL

Currently there are 0 customers online

Figure 108
The Tools Menu's
Who's Online Module

Chapter

17

Database &
Records Management

In this chapter:

Having a records backup in case of disaster is always important, but it's even more important when your store's records may be far away on the Internet. What would you do if you suddenly could not get to your store for a few days, or even forever? This chapter should help you plan for disaster, and hopefully prevent it.

Level of difficulty: easy and important for every store owner.

Unless you have led a charmed life, you have probably had to deal with a computer crash and loss of data at least once. If so, you are probably aware of how difficult it is to reconstruct your records.

Operating your store on the Internet adds another level of vulnerability. Not only could your own computer go out, but a connection along the way – your ISP, your telephone company, your web host – could go out, leaving you stranded and unable to operate your store. This is in addition to the possibility that your database simply becomes corrupt, for whatever reason.

This is not intended to scare you, but you must be aware of the risks in order to guard against them. If you have a regular records and database management program in place, you can rest easy.

Creating a disaster policy

How do you create a "disaster policy" unique for your store – a policy to cover most disaster scenarios? You stage your own disaster, and see what you need to be able to respond to it properly.

NOTE: This is not intended to be an all-inclusive list of disasters. You must gauge your own situation and your own risk.

Pretend that each of these disasters has happened to you. How could you prevent it? How can you respond?

Possible disaster scenarios:[‡]
1.   Your computer crashes, never to work again. You will spend a month reconstructing it.
2.   Your computer works, but the hard disk has failed. It may be recoverable.
3.   The electricity goes out for a minute... a day... 4 days.
4.   You forget to pay your dial-up or broadband ISP carrier, and they temporarily turn off your service. Whoops!
5.   Your osCommerce installer or programmer (or you) has a bad day, fails to make a backup copy before making just one little the site, and now all you can see is PARSE ERROR on your website—nothing more.

[‡] Believe it or not, I've had most or all of these things happen to me. Thankfully I have faithfully followed my own disaster policy. As they say, if you live long enough you will have a few scars, but it sure beats the alternative.

6. Your osCommerce web host has a server die, and they were not following their own backup policy. Their most recent copy, however, is several weeks old. You have lost weeks worth of orders.

7. Your osCommerce web host, who was always so nice and charming before, goes insane, makes a personal vendetta against you, and threatens to turn off your website.

8. Your osCommerce web host had to fire an employee who left with passwords. The ex-employee messes with your store and several others, corrupting your database.

9. Your osCommerce web host uses the same password naming scheme for all websites, and doesn't tell you how to change it. A client or employee with a grudge gets in and messes up your store.

10. Your osCommerce web host goes out of business, simply disappearing without a trace. No word; they simply are gone. Vanished!

Disaster Prevention:

1. Make regular backups of your personal computer AND your web host site. This can be totally automated for you with weekly full backups and daily backups of files that were changed. The backups should go on a SEPARATE read-only hard disk or other storage unit, not on the same one you use every day.

2. Get an Uninterruptible Power Supply (UPS) and have it set up properly and tested for you. This gives you approximately 3-5 minutes to shut down your computer in an orderly manner in case of a power outage, so you can save all your work.

3. Put your dialup or broadband ISP carrier on an automatic payment so you can't forget to pay them.

4. If you work on your own site, get in the habit of always making a duplicate and working on the duplicate file. If you use an installer or programmer, make sure you trust them. At the VERY first sign of sloppiness – like forgetting to make a backup before they work, look for a backup person who will not make that kind of mistake. Don't wait for two signs of sloppiness.

5. Do your homework, make sure you have a reliable osCommerce web host. They should have a stated "up-time" policy of 99% or more, and LIVE BY IT. If they have an outage, they should report it to you; you should NEVER discover it by yourself. If they make a mistake, they should admit it. If they blame you, it's time to move on.

6. Use careful password management. Use unhackable random passwords and change them frequently.

7. 7. Follow your own disaster policy!

Daily backups

Print a copy of EACH order as it comes in. Yes, it feels wasteful as you grind trees instead of electrons. But you can eventually recycle the paper, or use it as compost for planting more trees. This is the basis of your disaster plan; in case of a fire, flood, or other local emergency, you would grab your order binder and run.

An alternative is copying and pasting a copy of each order into a backup directory of your computer. But this is not portable in case of fire, tornado or other local emergency.

To print a copy of each orders, from the main Administrative Module screen, select **Customers** and then click the **VIEW** button.

Click the **EDIT** button to see the order, then **PRINT.**

Keep the daily orders in a 3 ring binder, and keep the binder in a safe place. A fireproof vault off-site would not be out of the question. You should get in the habit of moving the older records – say 8 week old orders that you know have been shipped, received, and not returned – to permanent storage off-site.

Your personal computer should be backed up daily with an "incremental" backup. This means each record that has been changed, is backed up. There are many back-up programs out there, even free ones, that can totally automate this process for you.

DOUBLE-CHECK regularly to make sure your daily backups are actually happening! You may think that they are scheduled and occurring, but a power outage or other event could cause it to change. Make sure you SEE your backups with your own eyes.

Weekly backups

You need a full digital backup of the database and website, AND your personal computer each week. You will need to do this in three phases:

1. Copy the database to your personal computer.
2. GET or SYNCHRONIZE your website to your personal computer.
3. BACKUP your personal computer.

Please follow the database backup instructions in the Website Housekeeping chapter. It is extremely easy to make backups, and takes only a minute or two.

Regular Testing

Once you get these systems working, it is critical that you periodically test them. These tests should be performed at least monthly, AFTER your site is stable. If you have any sign that it is not, and during the implementation phase when you are starting these disaster prevention steps, these tests should be performed even more frequently.

1. Is your Uninterruptible Power Supply working?

2. Do your automatic daily and weekly backups exist?

3. Does your ISP have the new expiration date on your credit card?

4. Are you satisfied with the reliability of your web host? Have they given you any signs that you should be concerned?

5. Have you followed your password policy and kept unhackable random passwords in a safe place?

6. Have you and your programmer followed your own backup policy and always worked on a copy of a file?

7. Have you run through the Possible Disaster Scenarios and developed your own?

Chapter 18

Bells & Whistles

In this chapter:

osCommerce add-ons can customize your site and make it easier to manage. They are called "contributions" because they are contributed on an 'as-is' basis for free by programmers for the joy of creating. Ask your installer to find the right contribution for your needs and to install it for you.

Level of difficulty: medium to difficult.

OS Commerce Add-Ons

Your installer should install these packages for you. Do not attempt it unless you know what you are doing. These modules should only be installed after your website is backed up, tested and stable.
CAUTION: Follow directions exactly, this is easy to mess up!
BE SURE TO MAKE A BACKUP FIRST!

TIP: Full instructions for installing the most popular contributions can be found in the companion book, the osCommerce TECHNICAL Manual oscommercemanuals.com.

You can find a list of available add-ons on the osCommerce website at
http://www.oscommerce.com/community/contributions/

The Contributions Listing on the osCommerce website with some popular sample items in each:

This contributions list is located on the osCommerce website at
http://www.oscommerce.com/community/contributions/

CREDIT MODULES: Discounts, County Sales Tax, Gift Voucher, Cross-Sell	# Contributions	**FEATURES:** Add Gift Registry/Wish List, Ad Tracker, Thumbnails, Memberships/ Subscriptions, Must agree to terms, more.

CREDIT MODULES:
Discounts, County Sales Tax, Gift Voucher, Cross-Sell

IMAGES:
Buttons and graphics.

LANGUAGES:
From A-Z, many with button packs.

PAYMENT:
Alternate processors such as AnyPay, International COD, etc.

SHIPPING:
Additional shipping options, Airborne Express, China Post, DHL, more.

ZONES:
Add more zones from Argentina to Venezuela.

Contributions

Contributions are provided by the community which are i form of project add-ons, feature updates, language pack: extended modules.

All contributed work is freely available under the GNU Ge Public License.

Downloads are hosted at SunSite.dk and Pair.

➤ Credit Modules
67 Packages

➤ Images
132 Packages

➤ Languages
105 Packages

➤ Payment Modules
218 Packages

➤ Shipping Modules
103 Packages

➤ Zones
52 Packages

➤ Features
516 Packages

➤ InfoBoxes
115 Packages

➤ Order Total Module
19 Packages

➤ Reports
21 Packages

➤ Templates/Theme:
32 Packages

➤ Other
178 Packages

Figure 109
osCommerce Website Listing
Contributions Currently Available

FEATURES:
Add Gift Registry/Wish List, Ad Tracker, Thumbnails, Memberships/ Subscriptions, Must agree to terms, more.

INFOBOXES:
Add to Favorites, Live Chat, Header Images, Viewed Products, Random Quotes, Tell a Friend, more.

ORDER TOTAL:
Shipping Insurance, Payment Type Surcharge, Zip-based sales tax

REPORTS:
Low Stock , Sales, Unsold Carts, Visitor Web Stats

TEMPLATES/ THEMES:
Skins, Set column widths, Simple Template System.

OTHER:
Access db to mySQL, Add Custom Message, Admin Login, Multiple Product move, copy, delete, Feedback Request, Import Tool for CSV Files, Printable Catalog, more.

DO NOT MIX contributions made for previous versions of osCommerce, that's like an electronic cocktail, you don't know WHAT IT WILL DO! Dates after July 2003 are USUALLY OKAY but check to be certain.

General directions for installing contributions:

1. MAKE SURE YOUR SITE IS BACKED UP, TESTED AND STABLE.
2. Make sure the contribution is made for the exact version of osCommerce you are using. DO NOT MIX VERSIONS.
3. Download the contribution file to your computer, and unzip.
4. Before you alter any pages in your website, make a COPY of the original page so you can revert back if necessary. Assume that you WILL have to revert at least once.
5. Read the README file and follow the instructions.
6. For instructions on installing the most popular contributions, get the osCommerce TECHNICAL manual at www.oscommercemanuals.com.
7. To receive technical assistance on add-ons, visit the CONTRIBUTIONS forum at <u>http://forums.oscommerce.com/</u>

APPENDIX A
osCommerce Installers,
Web Hosts & Consultants

Pithy Productions , Inc. http://www.pithyproductions.com/

Have you messed up your osCommerce site beyond repair? Stumped about an issue? Troubleshooting difficult installations is our specialty. We can fix your store and have it live again in as little as 24 hours. Ask an Expert service gives you quick answers to difficult osCommerce issues. We also do fully custom websites that include an online osCommerce store with installation and one year of free web hosting included.

McGinTech http://www.mcgintech.com/

Build Your Own osCommerce Package" includes a comprehensive list of the most popular contributions installed free or for a modest fee. McGinTech specializes in osCommerce design, hosting and template integration.

AABox Web Hosting http://www.aabox.com

Specializing in high-quality, low cost ecommerce hosting with FREE installation of standard osCommerce, osCommerce MAX MS2.2, contribution installation, FREE move from another site, and more. By the maker of osCommerce MAX MS2.2 and creator of www.oscdox.com, a popular forum and documentation site with separate forums for standard osCommerce and for MAX.

Hyperactive Co. www.hyperactivehosting.com

Owned and operated by Clifton Murphy, Author of the Linkpoint Payment Gateway for OS Commerce. We offer full service template design, custom PHP development and modifications at discount prices, usually $49.95 standard fee for module installations with 50% off if you host with us! We specialize in OS Commerce hosting plans and are an authorized reseller for both Linkpoint and Authorize.net, offering every service for your store under one roof.

osTemplates http://www.ostemplates.net

osTemplates is your one stop shop for all your osCommerce needs, including Template Integration, Contribution Installations, Custom add-ons, Search engine optimization and much more.

Help Desk Genius http://www.helpdeskgenius.com/

Hosting from $2.50 per month, includes instant self-service setup. Support services, custom osCommerce programming.

Chain Reaction Web http://www.chainreactionweb.com/

Free osCommerce installation on full access php hosting account. 35 contribution options included. Real full time support for use or support issues via phone or email 24/7 from the makers of the CRE loaded 6 osCommerce. Free SSL Server Access and free HTTPS

B2Services http://www.b2services.com/

With over 300 stores built on osCommerce and 15 employees B2Services is the leader in osCommerce services with a huge selection of add-on modules, design templates and services such as search engine optimization, html email, ebay add-on and a lot more. B2Services provides custom development and hosting for osCommerce as well.

Website Solution Limited http://www.website-solution.net

Specialized in osCommerce customizations & beautifications. Get rid of the boring OSC look - we can change your osCommerce shop to any look you want, just send us any HTML template and you can see your shop is right there!

Yourbizhosting.com Yourbizhosting.com

We load the MySql Database and osCommerce for the stores we host. We then password protect the admin section of the osCommerce software. We offer 4 hosting packages, each with dedicated ip addresses, ftp access, unlimited pop mail accounts, a graphical control panel for user ease. file managers, site stats, web building software, web mail and so much more.

APPENDIX B
List of Cheat Sheets Included with this Book

The following Cheat Sheets are available to our readers on the web at

http://www.pithyproductions.com/oscommerce/book/cheatsheets/

Cheat Sheet #1: <u>How to Make the Most of This Book</u>
Your cram sheet for squeezing everything you can from this publication.
Not available on the web.

Cheat Sheet #2: <u>PRE-SETUP Checklist for Your Store</u>
52 nitty gritty items that your installer might otherwise have to ask you one at a time.
Charts for colors, font sizes and styles. Emails results to you or your installer.

Cheat Sheet #3: <u>InfoBox Checklist</u>
Goes through every info box on the site from top to bottom and left to right, making sure
you are satisfied with the wording and contents of each one. Emails results to you or your
installer.

Cheat Sheet #4: <u>Greetings and Menubars Checklist</u>
Goes through every greeting and menu bar, making sure you are satisfied with the
wording and contents of each one. Emails results to you or your installer.

Cheat Sheet #5: <u>Stylesheet Cheatsheet for Programmers</u>
This is a fully-commented style sheet that programmers can upload directly to the website
to make style changes a breeze.

Cheat Sheet #6: <u>Advanced Users' Cheat Sheet</u>
A picture's worth a thousand words, and this annotated picture of an osCommerce
website tells you at a glance the shortcut to quickly editing each piece of the osCommerce
website.

INDEX

NOW AVAILABLE IN ELECTRONIC FORMAT

This book is also available in electronic book format
with full color screen shots and 100% searchable text.

For more information or to download your copy,
please visit our website at
http://www.osCommerceManuals.com.

PURCHASE THE COMPANION BOOK,
THE OSCOMMERCE TECHNICAL MANUAL

For those who wish to install, configure and customize their own
osCommerce websites. Available in both electronic e-Book and paperback
formats.

For more information or to download your copy,
please visit our website at
http://www.osCommerceManuals.com.

For information on obtaining mass quantities of this book
or joining our reseller program, visit our website at
http://www.osCommerceManuals.com.

ondemandmanuals.com
A division of Trafford Holdings Ltd.

Suite 6E, 2333 Government St., Victoria, BC V8T 4P4, Canada
Phone 250.383.6864 • Toll-free 888.232.4444 (Canada & US) Fax 250.383.6804
New Bern, NC, USA • Crewe, UK • Drogheda, County Louth, Ireland
E-mail sales@trafford.com • Web www.ondemandmanuals.com

This book was published *on-demand* in cooperation with OnDemandManuals.com and Trafford Publishing.

On-demand publishing is a unique process and service of making a book available for retail sale to the public taking advantage of on-demand manufacturing and Internet marketing.

On-demand publishing includes promotions, retail sales, manufacturing, order fulfilment, accounting and collecting royalties on behalf of the author.

Order Information:

Catalogue #04-1630

This book can be ordered online at www2.ondemandmanuals.com/pithyproductions. You can also order by phone or fax using the contact information above. Be sure to provide your name, address, phone number, email address, delivery instructions, credit card information, and catalogue number when placing your order.

ISBN 1412038815-4

9 781412 038157